T0012238

# BRAIN
# GAMES
### for
# 10 Year Olds

Puzzles and solutions
by Dr. Gareth Moore
BSc (Hons), MPhil, PhD

Illustrations and cover
artwork by Chris Dickason

Designed by Imago Create

# BRAIN GAMES
## for
# 10 Year Olds

Fun and Challenging
Brain Teasers, Logic Puzzles,
and More for Gritty Kids

ULYSSES BOOKS
**FOR YOUNG READERS**

Puzzles and solutions © 2024 Gareth Moore

Illustrations and layouts © 2024 Buster Books

Published in the United States by
ULYSSES BOOKS FOR YOUNG READERS,
an imprint of Ulysses Press
PO Box 3440
Berkeley, CA 94703
www.ulyssespress.com

First published as *Brain Games for Clever 10 Year Olds* in Great Britain in 2024 by Buster Books, an imprint of Michael O'Mara Books Limited

ISBN: 978-1-64604-691-1

2 4 6 8 10 9 7 5 3 1

# INTRODUCTION

Get ready to push your brain to the limit with these fun-filled games!

Take your pick of 101 puzzles. You can complete them in any order you like and work through at your own pace.

Start each puzzle by reading the instructions. Sometimes this is the hardest part of the puzzle, so don't worry if you have to read the instructions a few times to be clear on what they mean.

Once you know what to do, it's time to battle your way to the answer. Time yourself completing each puzzle, and write your time in the box at the top of each page. For an extra challenge, you can come back to the puzzles at a later date and see if you can complete them even faster.

There's a notes and scribbles section in the back that you can use to help you work out the answers.

If you really struggle with a puzzle, take a look at the solutions in the back to see how it works, then try it again later and see if you can work it out the second time around.

Good luck, and have fun!

## Introducing the Brain Games master:
## Gareth Moore, BSc (Hons), MPhil, PhD

Dr. Gareth Moore is a brain-games genius and author of lots of puzzle books.

He created an online brain-training site called BrainedUp.com, and runs a puzzle site called PuzzleMix.com. Gareth has a PhD from the University of Cambridge, where he taught machines to understand spoken English.

The names of four Olympic athletes have been disguised below, with the letters in each name shifted four places forward through the alphabet.

Decode each name by shifting each letter four places backward, so E becomes A, F becomes B and so on.

a) QMGLEIP TLIPTW

.................................................................................

b) YWEMR FSPX

.................................................................................

c) WMQSRI FMPIW

.................................................................................

d) RESQM SWEOE

.................................................................................

These six tiles can be swapped around to reveal a picture of a letter. What is that letter? You don't need to rotate any of the tiles.

The answer is: ............................................

Draw along the dashed lines to divide the grid into
dominoes so that there is exactly one of each type of
domino. Two have already been found to get you started.

a)

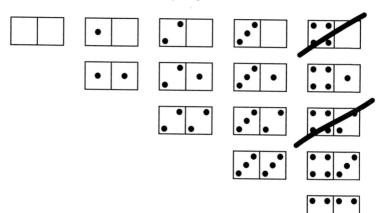

Cross each domino out as you find it:

In this second puzzle, numbers 0 to 4 are used instead of dots, but otherwise the puzzle solves in exactly the same way. Draw in borders so that there is exactly one of each type of domino.

b)

| 0 | 3 | 2 | 0 | 4 | 2 |
|---|---|---|---|---|---|
| 0 | 2 | 2 | 4 | 3 | 2 |
| 3 | 4 | 1 | 1 | 1 | 4 |
| 0 | 3 | 1 | 3 | 3 | 4 |
| 0 | 0 | 1 | 2 | 1 | 4 |

Use this table to keep track of the dominoes you have already found:

| 0 | 1 | 2 | 3 | 4 | |
|---|---|---|---|---|---|
| | | | | | 0 |
| | | | ✔ | | 1 |
| | | | | | 2 |
| | | | | | 3 |
| | | | | | 4 |

Can you circle the ten differences between these two images?

Imagine looking down on this arrangement of cubes from the direction of the arrow. Which of the options, *a* to *d*, would match what you see?

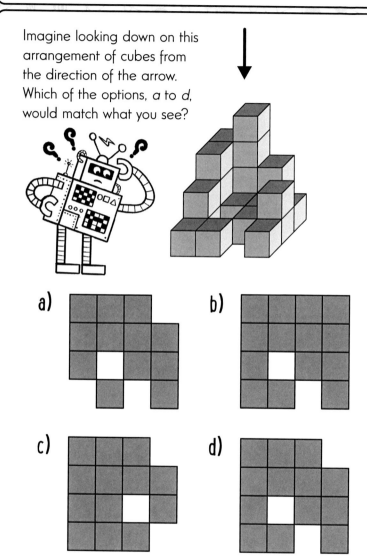

a)

b)

c)

d)

The answer is: ................................

Klimbits live on the planet Kook, where the currency is the klip (which is usually shortened to *k*). There are four types of klip coin on planet Kook:

a) What is the fewest number of klip coins that could be used to purchase a pet robot that costs 27k? The robot shop cannot give change, so you must make up exactly 27k using the coins.

.........................................................................................................

b) What is the fewest number of klip coins that could be used to purchase a space suit that costs 52k? The space-suit shop also cannot give change, so you must make up exactly 52k using the coins.

.........................................................................................................

c) On Kwibbledays you cannot use more than five of any one value of coin for a purchase. Today is a Kwibbleday, so what is the greatest number of coins that you could use to buy the 52k space suit? The shop still cannot give change, so you must make up exactly 52k.

.........................................................................................................

Can you fill in every empty block in each number pyramid so that each square contains a value equal to the sum of the two numbers directly beneath it?

Here's an example to show what a complete pyramid looks like:

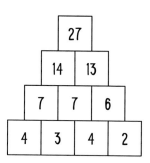

|  | 27 |  |
|---|---|---|
| | 14 | 13 |
| 7 | 7 | 6 |
| 4 | 3 | 4 | 2 |

a)

| 11 | 14 | 13 | 7 |

b)

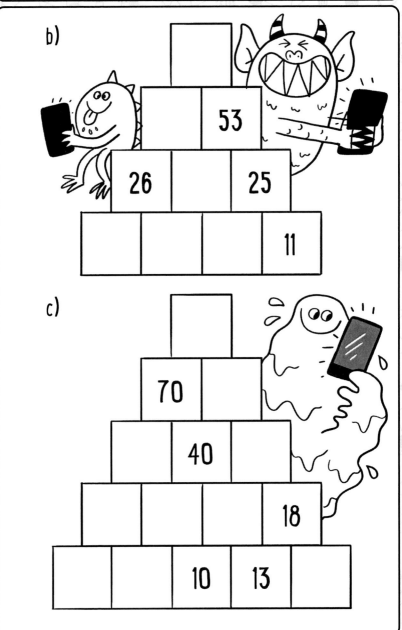

| | |
|---|---|
| | 53 |

| 26 | | 25 |

| | | | 11 |

c)

| 70 | |

| 40 | |

| | 18 |

| 10 | 13 |

Can you find each of these sixteen numbers in the grid?
They can be written in any direction, including diagonally,
and may read forward or backward.

| | | | |
|---|---|---|---|
| 12088 | 232233 | 642329 | 700544 |
| 138347 | 380491 | 671855 | 704814 |
| 191529 | 608529 | 678949 | 979016 |
| 216083 | 61662 | 679333 | 98848 |

| | | | | | | | | | | | | |
|---|---|---|---|---|---|---|---|---|---|---|---|---|
| 4 | 1 | 1 | 8 | 2 | 3 | 4 | 3 | 8 | 0 | 6 | 1 | 2 | 3 |
| 9 | 9 | 2 | 5 | 8 | 0 | 6 | 1 | 9 | 4 | 4 | 6 | 7 | 6 |
| 1 | 3 | 8 | 3 | 4 | 7 | 3 | 5 | 5 | 8 | 1 | 7 | 6 | 7 |
| 2 | 6 | 2 | 9 | 7 | 3 | 8 | 7 | 0 | 0 | 5 | 4 | 4 | 9 |
| 0 | 1 | 8 | 7 | 9 | 4 | 3 | 9 | 0 | 1 | 6 | 1 | 4 | 3 |
| 3 | 6 | 2 | 8 | 8 | 4 | 6 | 3 | 1 | 2 | 9 | 9 | 4 | 6 |
| 4 | 6 | 3 | 8 | 0 | 7 | 9 | 3 | 9 | 9 | 8 | 5 | 6 | 6 |
| 2 | 2 | 9 | 8 | 0 | 2 | 3 | 3 | 0 | 7 | 4 | 9 | 8 | 9 |
| 5 | 4 | 2 | 4 | 5 | 2 | 1 | 8 | 6 | 8 | 6 | 0 | 3 | 8 |
| 0 | 2 | 8 | 1 | 2 | 3 | 0 | 8 | 8 | 9 | 5 | 3 | 8 | 8 |
| 9 | 1 | 9 | 3 | 7 | 9 | 9 | 7 | 6 | 2 | 6 | 6 | 6 | 3 |
| 4 | 1 | 2 | 3 | 9 | 7 | 9 | 0 | 1 | 6 | 3 | 4 | 8 | 4 |
| 0 | 4 | 1 | 0 | 3 | 9 | 9 | 2 | 4 | 0 | 2 | 3 | 3 | 3 |
| 0 | 4 | 7 | 6 | 1 | 0 | 3 | 9 | 2 | 3 | 2 | 4 | 6 | 4 |

Take a look at the sequence below, then work out which of the options, *a* to *e*, should replace the empty box to complete the sequence.

a)

b)

c)

d)

e)

The answer is: ........................................

BRAIN GAME 10 ⟶     ⏰ TIME ........................................

Cross out exactly one digit in each of the following incorrect calculations so that they become correct. For example, 12 + 3 = 4 would be correct if you crossed out the *2* so it read 1 + 3 = 4.

8 + 18 = 206

73 + 54 = 1275

100 × 20 = 200

32 + 43 + 54 = 1239

742 ÷ 12 = 6

How many rectangles, of various sizes, can you count in the picture below? Don't forget the large one all around the outside!

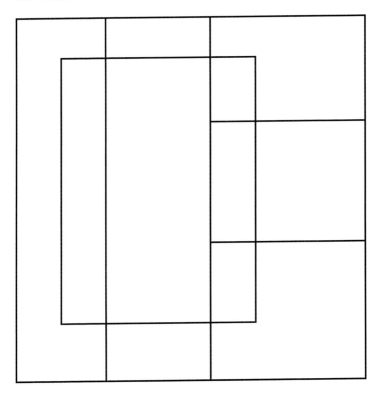

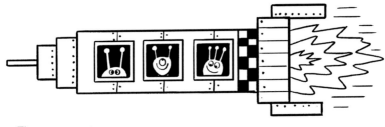

The answer is: ................................

Draw along the dashed lines to create fences that divide each of these grids into a set of square fields, just like in the example below. Every field must contain exactly one monster, and every grid square must be part of exactly one field.

Take a look at this example to see how this works:

a)

b)

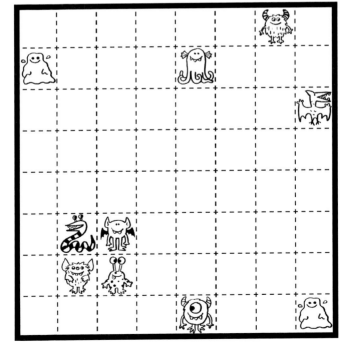

Find the shortest route from the entrance to the exit, without backtracking. What is the total of all the numbers that this shortest route passes through?

One of the following images is not like the others. Which one, and why?

a)

b)

c)

d)

e)

f)

The answer is: ........................ because ...............................................................

....................................................................................................................

Write a letter from A to F into each empty square so that no letter repeats in any row or column. Also, identical letters cannot be in touching squares—not even diagonally.

Here's an example solved puzzle, to show how it works:

| C | F | D | B | E | A |
|---|---|---|---|---|---|
| E | B | A | C | D | F |
| D | C | F | E | A | B |
| A | E | B | D | F | C |
| F | D | C | A | B | E |
| B | A | E | F | C | D |

a)

| | A | | | C | |
|---|---|---|---|---|---|
| B | C | | | D | F |
| | | | | | |
| | | | | | |
| D | F | | | B | C |
| | B | | | A | |

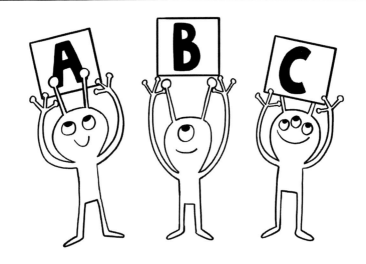

b)

| | | B | A | | |
|---|---|---|---|---|---|
| | A | | | F | |
| F | | | | | C |
| C | | | | | E |
| | D | | | B | |
| | | F | D | | |

Pablo and Quinn are sending letters to each other over the summer holidays. Pablo mails a letter on Monday, and Quinn receives it two days later. Quinn then sends a letter back to Pablo the day after receiving Pablo's letter, which Pablo receives three days later.

a) On what day did Pablo receive his letter?

........................................................................................

If both letters had taken twice as long to arrive, then:

b) How many days after initially mailing his letter would Pablo have received his reply from Quinn?

........................................................................................

c) What day of the week would that have been?

........................................................................................

You're helping to build a robot and need a specific set of parts. Spend as long as you need to memorize the following list of words. Then, when you think you will remember all of the items on the list, turn the page and follow the instructions there.

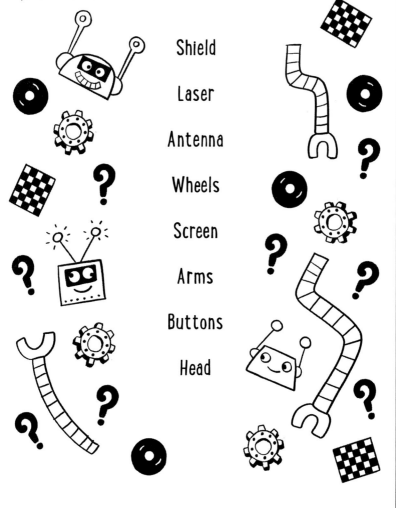

Shield

Laser

Antenna

Wheels

Screen

Arms

Buttons

Head

Here is the same list of parts again, but this time in a different order and with three items missing. Can you write in all of the missing items?

**Buttons**

**Head**

**Screen**

**Shield**

**Wheels**

Which three parts are missing?

.........................................................................................................................

.........................................................................................................................

.........................................................................................................................

Starting on a circle that contains a 1, can you trace a route along the lines to 2, 3, 4, 5 and then 6 in that order, without visiting any number more than once?

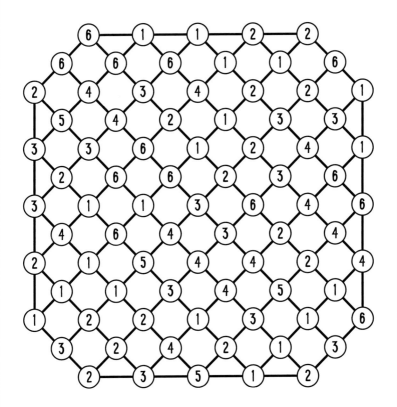

Draw lines to join each pair of identical shapes, just like in the example solution below. Only one line can enter each square, and lines can't be drawn diagonally.

Here's an example solved puzzle, so you can see how it works:

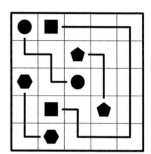

a)

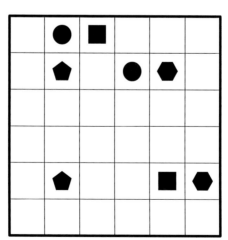

b)

c)

⏱ TIME _____

For each of the three given totals, can you pick one number from each of the rings so that they add up to that total? For example, you could form a total of 9 by picking 4 from the innermost ring, 3 from the middle ring, and 2 from the outermost ring.

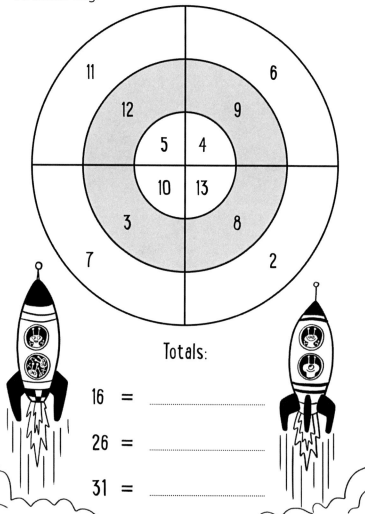

Totals:

16 = _____

26 = _____

31 = _____

Each of these two pictures shows the same background image, but in each case different parts of it are covered by white squares. By imagining combining the two pictures, so the empty squares on one are replaced with the corresponding squares from the other picture, can you answer the following questions?

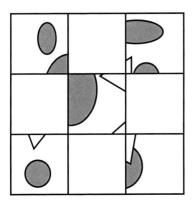

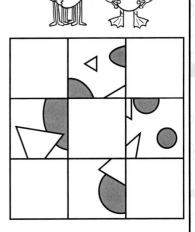

a) How many shaded ellipses (ovals and circles) are there in the combined image?

.................................................................................................................................

b) How many triangles are there in the combined image?

.................................................................................................................................

c) How many of the triangles overlap with a shaded ellipse?

.................................................................................................................................

Write a digit from 1 to 6 into each empty square so that no digit repeats in any row, column or bold-lined 3x2 box.

Here's an example solved puzzle, to show how it works:

| 1 | 2 | 4 | 5 | 3 | 6 |
|---|---|---|---|---|---|
| 3 | 5 | 6 | 1 | 2 | 4 |
| 5 | 1 | 3 | 6 | 4 | 2 |
| 6 | 4 | 2 | 3 | 1 | 5 |
| 2 | 3 | 5 | 4 | 6 | 1 |
| 4 | 6 | 1 | 2 | 5 | 3 |

a)

6
4
2

| | | | | | |
|---|---|---|---|---|---|
| | 6 | 5 | 2 | 3 | |
| | 4 | 1 | 5 | 2 | |
| | 2 | 6 | 1 | 4 | |
| | 5 | 3 | 6 | 1 | |
| | | | | | |

3
5
1

b)

**4 3 1** (left) / **2 6 5** (right)

| 1 |   | 5 | 4 |   | 6 |
|---|---|---|---|---|---|
|   |   |   |   |   |   |
| 2 |   | 1 | 3 |   | 5 |
| 6 |   | 3 | 1 |   | 4 |
|   |   |   |   |   |   |
| 4 |   | 2 | 6 |   | 1 |

c)

**5 1 6** (left) / **3 4 2** (right)

|   | 1 |   |   |   |   |
|---|---|---|---|---|---|
|   |   | 4 | 5 |   | 3 |
|   |   |   |   |   | 4 |
| 6 |   |   |   |   |   |
| 5 |   | 6 | 3 |   |   |
|   |   |   |   | 6 |   |

Imagine that you cut out and then fold up (bending the paper away from you) the following picture to make a six-sided cube:

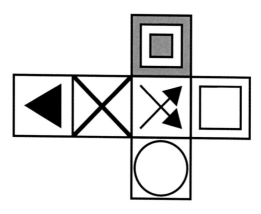

Without actually making the cube, can you say which of the following images would be a possible view of the resulting cube?

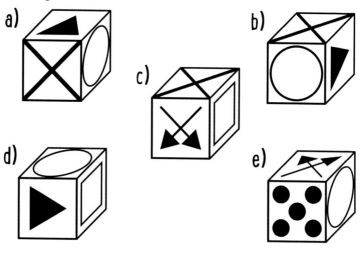

a)

b)

c)

d)

e)

The answer is: .....................

Asif, Bobby and Clara are all different ages. You also know that:

- Clara is half of Bobby's age

- In two years, Bobby will be twice as old as Asif is now

- One year ago, Asif was the same age as Clara is now

- The youngest of the three is four years old

Now can you work out how old each child is? Write your answers in the spaces below:

Asif: ......................................................

Bobby: ......................................................

Clara: ......................................................

Some monsters are hiding in each of these grids.
Can you find them all?

- None of the monsters are in the grid squares with numbers

- There is never more than one monster per grid square

- Numbers reveal the total number of monsters in
  all touching squares—including diagonally
  touching squares

Look at this solved puzzle
to see how this works:

| 1 | | (monster) |
|---|---|---|
| (monster) | 3 | 2 |
| 1 | 2 | (monster) |

a)

| 1 | 2 | | |
|---|---|---|---|
| | | 4 | |
| 2 | | | 3 |
| | 2 | 3 | |

b)

| 1 |   | 2 | 1 |
|---|---|---|---|
|   | 3 |   | 2 |
| 2 |   | 3 |   |
|   | 2 |   | 1 |

c)

| 1 | 3 |   | 4 |   |
|---|---|---|---|---|
|   |   |   | 4 |   |
|   |   | 2 | 4 | 2 |
| 2 | 3 |   |   |   |
|   |   | 1 | 2 | 1 |

Lucy has a pencil case containing pencils of four different shades. It contains:

- Four red pencils

- Six blue pencils

- Nine green pencils

- Five yellow pencils

If Lucy picks a pencil at random from her pencil case, without looking, then how many—and which—of the following statements will be true? Assume that all the pencils feel exactly the same to the touch and there are no other items in her pencil case.

a) Lucy is twice as likely to pick out a green pencil as a yellow pencil

b) Lucy is most likely to pick out a green pencil

c) The chance of Lucy picking a blue pencil is 1 in 4, or 25%

d) Lucy is more likely to pick out a yellow pencil than a blue pencil

e) Lucy is least likely to pick out a red pencil

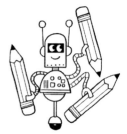

The answer is: ..........................................................

You have the following key on your key ring, but aren't sure which door it opens. Which one of the lock profiles shown beneath does it fit? Circle the correct one.

a) ▮▮ ▮ ▮▮▮

b) ▮ ▮ ▮ ▮▮

c) ▮▮▮ ▮▮▮

d) ▮▮▮ ▮▮▮

e) ▮▮ ▮▮ ▮

f) ▮▮▮ ▮▮▮

Imagine that you have placed 64 bricks to form a 4x4x4 cube, so they look like this:

**a)** You then take some bricks away to leave the following picture. How many bricks remain in this arrangement? None of them are floating.

The answer is: ......................................

**b)** You then put all the bricks back so there are 64 of them again. Now you remove some more again to leave the following arrangement. How many bricks are left this time?

The answer is: ...................................

Paola, Jack and Meera are all painting pictures. They are each painting a different object, using a different type of paint.

- Jack is using oil paints

- One of the painters is using finger paints

- One of the paintings is of a flower

- Paola is painting a monster

- The person painting a seashell is using acrylic paints

Given the information above, now work out:

a) What type of paint is Paola using? _____

b) What picture is Jack painting? _____

c) Which of the three is using acrylic paints? _____

You can use the table below to help you keep track of your work:

| Person | Picture | Type of Paint |
|--------|---------|---------------|
| Paola  |         |               |
| Jack   |         |               |
| Meera  |         |               |

Take a good look at this picture, then when you think you will remember it, turn the page.

Circle the six changes to the picture. Try to do this without looking back.

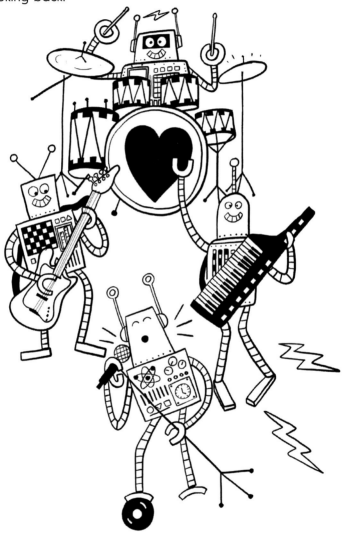

If you didn't find them all, look back and try again.

The names of six well-known authors have been disguised below. Can you crack the code and identify them all?

Hint: Think about the position of each letter in the alphabet!

a) 18-15-1-12-4   4-1-8-12

b) 10-21-4-25   2-12-21-13-5

c) 10-5-6-6 11-9-14-14-5-25

d) 10   11   18-15-23-12-9-14-7

e) 2-5-1-20-18-9-24   16-15-20-20-5-18

Once you understand how the code works, can you write down how BEVERLY CLEARLY should look in this code?

Write in numbers so that every square contains exactly one number, and each number from 1 to 16 appears once. Every square containing an arrow must point in the direction of the next square in numerical order—although that square might not be a touching square.

Take a look at this example solution to see how it works:

| 1 ↓ | 13 → | 14 → | 15 ↓ |
| 8 ↓ | 6 → | 5 ← | 7 ← |
| 9 → | 12 ↑ | 11 ← | 10 ← |
| 2 → | 3 → | 4 ↑ | 16 |

**a)**

| 1 ↓ | → | ↓ | 13 ↓ |
| 2 → | ↑ | 3 ↑ | ↓ |
| ↓ | ← | ← | 14 ↑ |
| → | 10 ↑ | ↑ | 16 |

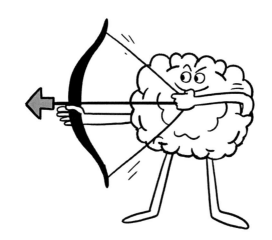

b)

| 1 → | ↓ | 2 ↓ | 15 ↓ |
|---|---|---|---|
| → | → | ← | 14 ↑ |
| ↓ | 4 → | ← | ← |
| → | ↑ | ← | 16 |

Write a letter from A to G into each empty square so that
no letter repeats in any row or column. Also, identical
letters cannot be in touching squares—not even diagonally.

Here's an example solved puzzle,
to show how it works:

| C | D | E | F | B | G | A |
|---|---|---|---|---|---|---|
| B | F | G | A | E | D | C |
| D | A | C | B | G | F | E |
| E | G | F | D | C | A | B |
| A | C | B | G | F | E | D |
| F | E | A | C | D | B | G |
| G | B | D | E | A | C | F |

a)

| | G | | | | D | |
|---|---|---|---|---|---|---|
| E | | | | | | C |
| | | B | | A | | |
| | | | D | | | |
| | | A | | E | | |
| A | | | | | | E |
| | C | | | | A | |

b)

| A | | F | | E | | C |
|---|---|---|---|---|---|---|
| | | | | | | |
| F | | | D | | | E |
| | | B | | A | | |
| C | | | F | | | B |
| | | | | | | |
| E | | G | | C | | D |

⏰ TIME ............................................

These nine tiles can be placed together into a 3x3 grid to reveal a picture of a letter. Can you use your imagination to rotate and assemble them?

The letter is: ............................................

Maria has a pet fish called Nick, who lives in a fish bowl. He spends all of this time swimming in circles, sometimes swimming in a clockwise direction and sometimes swimming in the opposite direction.

Maria watches Nick for half an hour, and notices that during that time Nick swims around the bowl exactly six times in a clockwise direction, and exactly twice in the opposite direction. Which of the following statements is true of this half hour?

a)  The number of swims around the bowl in the opposite direction is a quarter of the number of clockwise swims

b)  The number of swims around the bowl in the opposite direction is a third of the number of clockwise swims

c)  The number of swims around the bowl in the opposite direction is a half of the number of clockwise swims

.................................................................................................................

If Nick always behaved the same way for each half-hour period, then over a period of two and a half hours, how many clockwise loops of the bowl would Nick make?

.................................................................................................................

Draw horizontal and vertical lines to join all the dots into a single loop. Some of the dots are joined already to get you started. Each dot can be visited only once as you travel around the loop.

Here's an example solved puzzle to show you how it works:

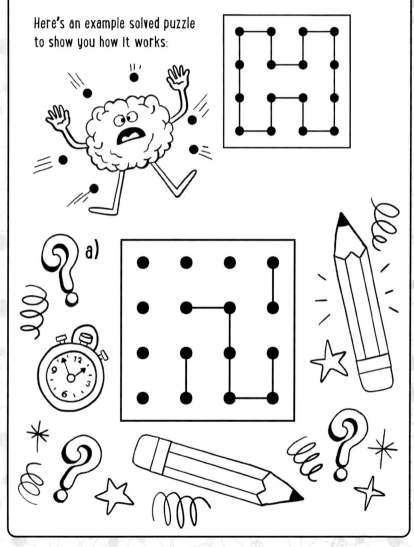

a)

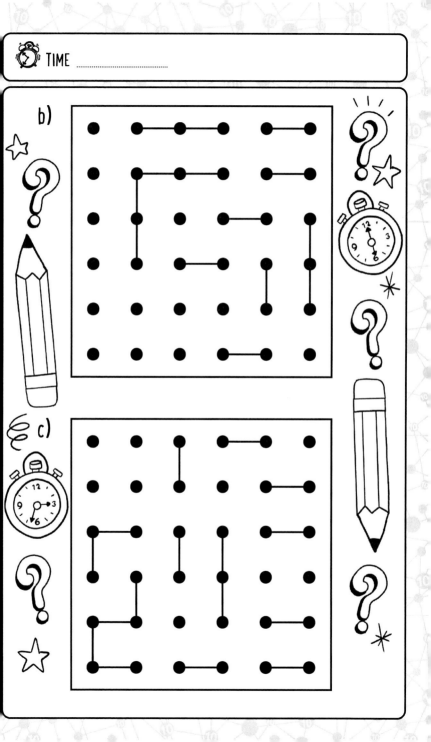

TIME ....................................

b)

c)

Complete each of these jigdoku puzzles by placing a letter from A to F into each empty square. Place letters so that:

- No letter repeats in any row or column

- No letter repeats within any bold-lined shape

This completed puzzle helps show how it works:

| D | F | C | A | B | E |
|---|---|---|---|---|---|
| C | B | A | E | D | F |
| F | A | B | D | E | C |
| A | E | D | F | C | B |
| B | D | E | C | F | A |
| E | C | F | B | A | D |

a)

| F | C |   |   | E |   |
|---|---|---|---|---|---|
|   |   |   |   | A |   |
|   |   | A | B | F | D |
| A | F | E | D |   |   |
|   | B |   |   |   |   |
|   | A |   |   | D | F |

b)

| E |   |   |   | D |   |
|---|---|---|---|---|---|
| C |   |   | E |   |   |
| F |   |   | A |   |   |
|   |   | C |   |   | D |
|   |   | E |   |   | A |
|   | F |   |   |   | E |

Imagine that you cut out and then fold up each of these images to make four six-sided cubes:

a)

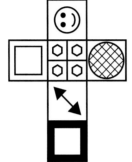

b)

c)

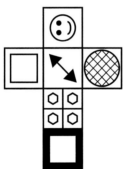

d)

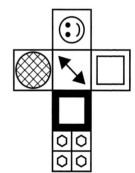

Which one of the options, a to d, would match this assembled cube?

The answer is: ........................

A mathematical transformation has been hidden in each of these central squares, marked with a ? Can you work out what is going on in each puzzle to change the circled numbers into the numbers inside the triangles, following the straight-line path of each arrow?

a)

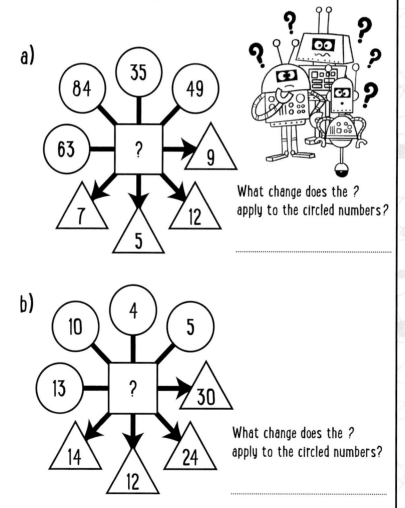

What change does the ? apply to the circled numbers?

........................................

b)

What change does the ? apply to the circled numbers?

........................................

Can you draw a loop that visits every white square once each? The loop can't visit any square more than once, or visit a shaded square. This also means that it can't cross itself.

Take a look at this example to see how this works:

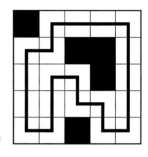

a)

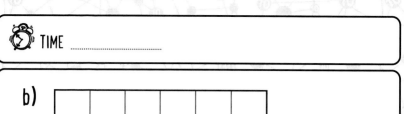
b)

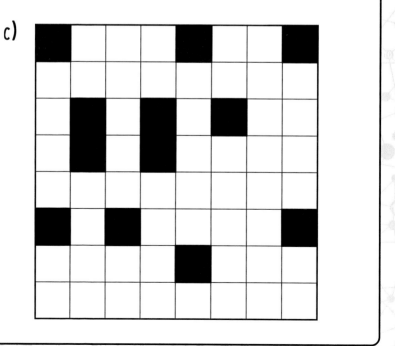

c)

Draw along the dashed lines to divide the grid up into regions that each contain exactly one of every letter.

Take a look at this example solved puzzle to see how this works:

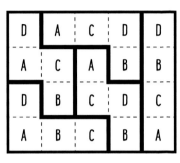

In the first puzzle, divide the grid into four regions that each contain one of every letter from A to D.

a)

| C | D | C | B | A |
|---|---|---|---|---|
| B | D | A | D | C |
| D | A | A | A | B |
| B | C | B | C | D |

In the next two puzzles, divide the grid into seven regions that each contain one of every letter from A to E.

b)

| D | C | D | B | C | B | E |
|---|---|---|---|---|---|---|
| E | B | E | E | A | D | C |
| D | B | A | C | E | A | A |
| A | C | A | D | D | B | E |
| B | E | C | C | D | A | B |

c)

| C | A | B | C | A | C | A |
|---|---|---|---|---|---|---|
| D | E | E | D | A | E | B |
| B | D | B | E | C | D | D |
| C | B | E | C | D | E | A |
| D | A | A | B | B | E | C |

 TIME ............................

Which number should come next in each of the following mathematical sequences?

**a)** 4096   1024   256   64   16   ..................

**b)** 226   207   188   169   150   ..................

**c)** 567   690   813   936   1059   ..................

**d)** 19   28   37   46   55   ..................

**e)** 1   2   6   24   120   ..................

**f)** 97   89   83   79   73   ..................

Tip: 'f' is tricky! What property do all these numbers share?

One of the following images is not like the others. Which one, and why?

**a)**

**b)**

**c)**

**d)**

**e)**

**f)**

The answer is: ........................... because ...............................................................

...............................................................................................................................................

Place either a *0* or a *1* into every empty square, so that every row and column contains equal numbers of each digit. Also, you cannot ever have more than two of the same digit next to each other when reading along a row or column. So *1* and *11* are both okay, but *111* would not be allowed.

Take a look at this example to see how it works. Notice how each row and each column contains two *1*'s and two *0*'s:

| 0 | 1 | 0 | 1 |
|---|---|---|---|
| 1 | 0 | 0 | 1 |
| 1 | 0 | 1 | 0 |
| 0 | 1 | 1 | 0 |

Now try this puzzle:

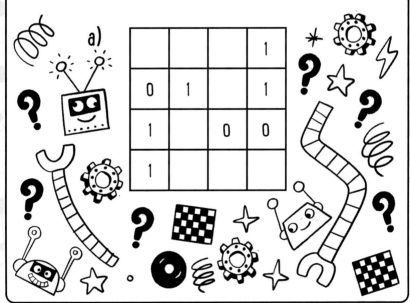

a)

|   |   |   | 1 |
|---|---|---|---|
| 0 | 1 |   | 1 |
| 1 |   | 0 | 0 |
| 1 |   |   |   |

In these next two puzzles each row and column should contain three *0's* and three *1's*:

**b)**

|   |   |   |   |   |   |
|---|---|---|---|---|---|
|   |   | 1 |   | 1 | 1 |
| 0 | 0 |   |   | 1 |   |
|   |   | 0 |   |   | 0 |
| 0 |   |   | 0 |   |   |
|   | 0 |   |   | 0 | 0 |
| 1 | 1 |   | 1 |   |   |

**c)**

|   |   |   |   |   |   |
|---|---|---|---|---|---|
| 0 | 0 |   |   | 1 |   |
|   | 1 |   | 1 |   |   |
|   | 0 | 1 |   | 0 | 1 |
| 0 | 0 |   | 0 | 1 |   |
|   |   | 0 |   | 0 |   |
|   | 1 |   |   | 0 | 0 |

⏱ TIME ...........................................

The time in Tokyo is eight hours ahead of the time in London. That means that when it is midday in London, it is 8 p.m. in Tokyo.

**a)** If the time is currently 3 p.m. in Tokyo, what time is it in London?

.........................................................................................................................................

**b)** If the time is now 10 p.m. in London, what time is it in Tokyo?

.........................................................................................................................................

The time in Mexico City is seven hours behind the time in London.

**c)** How many hours ahead of Mexico City is Tokyo?

.........................................................................................................................................

**d)** If it's now 7 a.m. in Mexico City, which one of the following is true?

- It's 3 p.m. in London and 6 p.m. in Tokyo

- It's noon in London and midnight in Tokyo

- It's 2 p.m. in London and 10 p.m. in Tokyo

- It's 4 p.m. in London and 2 a.m. in Tokyo

.........................................................................................................................................

Can you draw along some of the dashed lines to divide this shape into four identical pieces, with no unused parts left over?

Each of the four pieces must be identical, although they can be rotated relative to one another.

Take a look at the solved example, to see how it works.

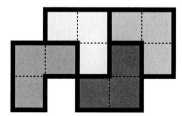

On the top of this puzzle are 36 coins. Your job is to pick them all up and find a route to one of the two exits by moving only along the marked paths. Every time you reach a stepping stone, you must drop 6 coins. By the time you reach the exit, you must have exactly 0 coins left. No stone can be visited more than once. You are not allowed to move to a stone if you have no coins left, so there is only one way to do this! Can you find the correct route?

36

Exit   Exit

The next day, you are asked to do the same job again, using the same paths and stepping stones—except that this time you drop only 4 coins on each stone. Again, you must start with 36 coins and must reach an exit with exactly 0 coins left. Can you find a new route that will allow you to do this?

## BRAIN GAME 48

TIME ..............................

Imagine looking down on this arrangement of cubes from the direction of the arrow. Which of the options, *a* to *d*, would match what you see?

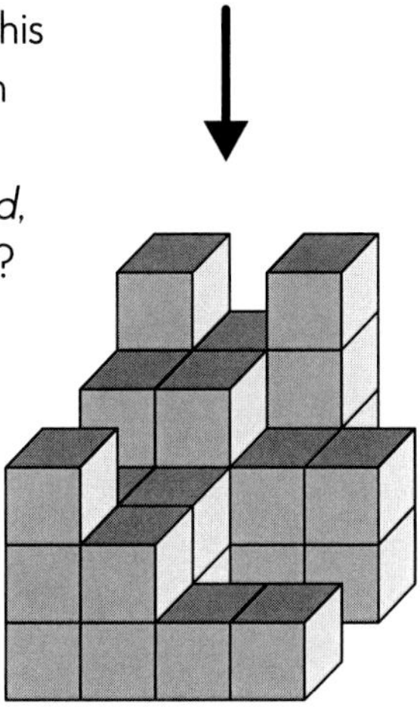

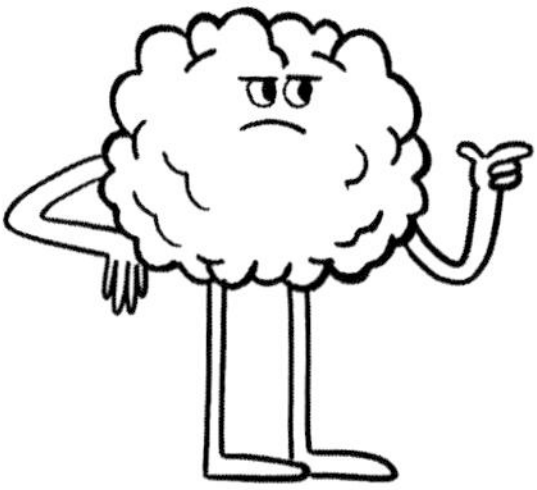

a)

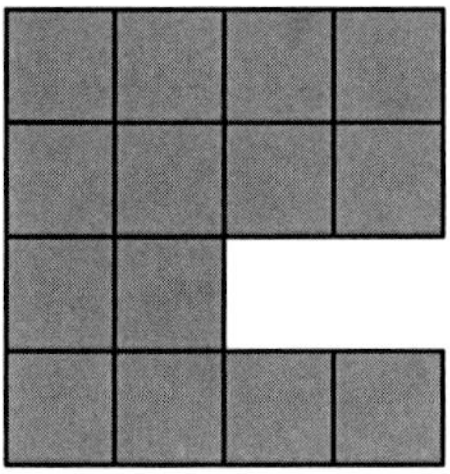

b)

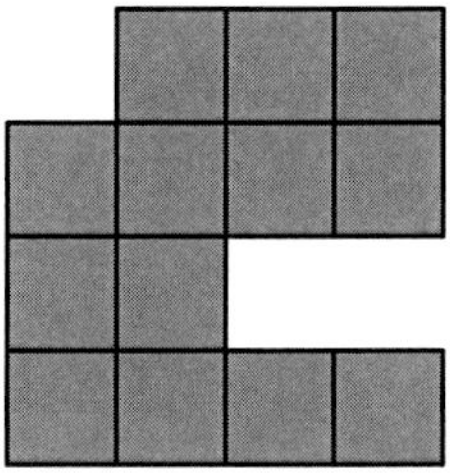

c)

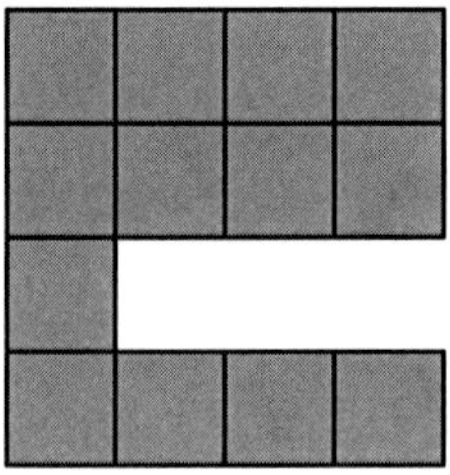

d)

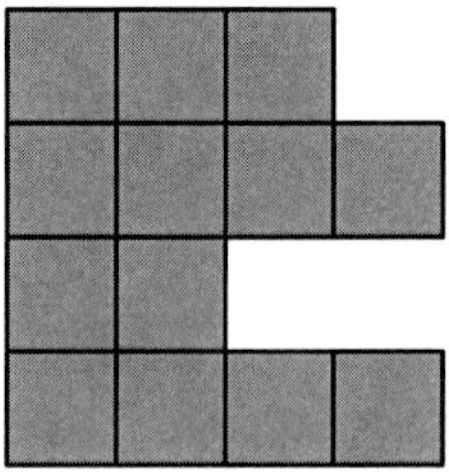

The answer is: ..............................

Zak is exactly one year and twenty days older than his brother Javid. Javid's birthday is on January 4th.

a) On what date is Zak's birthday?

............................................................................................................................

Zak has just turned eleven years old, and his birthday was on a Friday.

b) How many years old was Javid when Zak turned eleven?

............................................................................................................................

c) What day of the week will it be when Javid celebrates his next birthday?

............................................................................................................................

Can you circle the fifteen differences between these two images?

Place all of the given numbers into the grid, crossword-style, so that each number can be read once either across or down. Place one digit per square.

| 3 Digits | 4 Digits | 5 Digits | | 6 Digits | 7 Digits |
|----------|----------|----------|----------|----------|----------|
| 488 | 5333 | 29273 | 52447 | 179581 | 7423281 |
| 588 | 8455 | 31317 | 79297 | 582983 | 8139637 |
| | 8598 | 85561 | 85561 | 612656 | 9123918 |
| | 9424 | 51995 | 96248 | 881771 | 9312644 |

You're building a spaceship, and need the following list of parts in the quantities shown in the right-hand column. Spend a few minutes studying the list, and try to memorize both the parts needed as well as how many you need of each. Once you think you'll be able to recall them all, turn the page and follow the instructions there.

| | |
|---|---|
| Windows | 6 |
| Wings | 5 |
| Satellite launcher | 1 |
| Airlock doors | 4 |
| Air tanks | 6 |
| Alien portals | 3 |

Can you rewrite the list from the previous page by completing the missing parts and quantities?

**Windows** .....................................

..................................... 5

**Satellite launcher** .....................................

..................................... 4

**Air tanks** .....................................

..................................... 3

If you can't remember all the information, repeat the brain game until you have written them all in.

Femi, George and Hanna are all walking home from school together, along with Hanna's mom. They each live on the same road as their school, although their houses are not next door to one another.

- Walking directly home from school, it takes them three minutes to reach Femi's house, and he goes inside.

- Walking from Femi's house to George's house then takes twice as long as it did to reach Femi's house from school. George goes inside.

- Finally, Hanna and her mom walk the final stretch, which takes them two-thirds of the time it took to walk from Femi's house to George's house, plus an extra minute.

Now answer the following questions:

a) How long did it take for Hanna to walk home from school to her house, assuming that she didn't stop along the way?

.......................................................................................................

b) If Femi were to walk at the same speed as Hanna did, how long would it now take Femi to walk from his own house to Hanna's?

.......................................................................................................

Four views of the same cube are shown here, but one of the faces has been removed on the fourth cube:

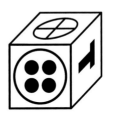

Which of the following five faces should replace the blank face to complete the cube correctly?

a)

b)

c)

d)

e)

The answer is: ........................................

Cross out one number in each of the following rows to create a mathematical number sequence. For example, if the numbers were 2 4 6 7 8 10, then you could cross out the 7 to create the sequence "add 2 at each step": 2 4 6 8 10.

a)   145     168     191     203     214     237

b)   243     121     81      27      9       3

c)   955     910     855     800     745     690

d)   100     75      50      33⅓     25      20

e)   1       5       25      125     375     625

Draw horizontal and vertical lines to join all the dots into a single loop. Some of the dots are joined already to get you started. Each dot can be visited only once as you travel around the loop.

Here's an example solved puzzle to show you how it works:

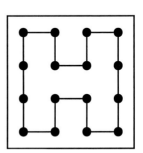

a)

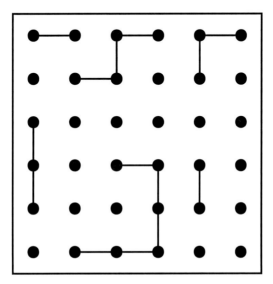

b)

⏱ TIME ........................................

Taken together, the two grids below conceal the name of a very famous person. Can you work out how to use them to reveal the name? It is up to you to work out how to do this!

| A | L | E | L | L | L |
|---|---|---|---|---|---|
| L | B | E | I | N | R |
| T | A | O | E | U | R |
| C | I | R | O | N | S |
| S | T | I | E | T | L |
| R | I | I | T | H | N |

Write the revealed person here:

............................................ ............................................

Blingertons live on the planet Blibble, where the currency is the blib (which is usually shortened to *b*. There are four types of blib coin on planet Blibble:

Bob the Blingerton has a wallet with some blib coins in it. He can see that:

- He has at least one of each value of blib coin

- He has no more than four of any value of blib coin

- He has a different quantity of each value of coin

- He has twice as many 5b coins as he has 14b coins

- The total value of the blib coins he has in his wallet is 74 blib

- He only has one 20b coin

Can you work out exactly which coins Bob has in his wallet?

............................................. x 2b          ............................................. x 5b

............................................. x 14b          ............................................. x 20b

Draw along the dashed lines to create fences that divide each of these grids into a set of square fields, just like in the example below. Every field must contain exactly one animal, and every grid square must be part of exactly one field.

Take a look at this example to see how this works:

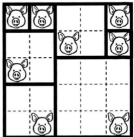

**a)**

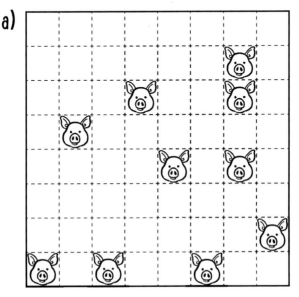

**b)**

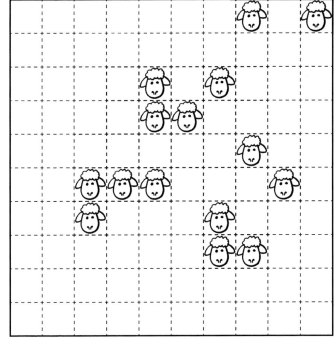

Write a digit from 1 to 9 into each empty square so that no digit repeats in any row, column or bold-lined 3x3 box.

a)

| 9 |   | 1 |   |   |   | 4 |   | 5 |
|---|---|---|---|---|---|---|---|---|
|   |   |   | 7 | 5 | 1 |   |   |   |
| 8 |   |   | 9 | 4 | 3 |   |   | 2 |
|   | 8 | 7 | 1 |   | 5 | 2 | 9 |   |
|   | 5 | 9 |   |   |   | 7 | 1 |   |
|   | 3 | 2 | 4 |   | 9 | 5 | 8 |   |
| 5 |   |   | 6 | 9 | 2 |   |   | 7 |
|   |   |   | 8 | 3 | 7 |   |   |   |
| 7 |   | 3 |   |   |   | 6 |   | 8 |

b)

|   | 8 | 9 | 5 |   | 6 | 7 | 1 |   |
|---|---|---|---|---|---|---|---|---|
| 4 |   |   |   | 1 |   |   |   | 8 |
| 7 |   |   | 2 |   | 8 |   |   | 5 |
| 3 |   | 4 |   |   |   | 5 |   | 1 |
|   | 5 |   |   |   |   |   | 3 |   |
| 6 |   | 2 |   |   |   | 4 |   | 9 |
| 1 |   |   | 8 |   | 7 |   |   | 4 |
| 8 |   |   |   | 2 |   |   |   | 7 |
|   | 9 | 7 | 4 |   | 1 | 8 | 6 |   |

⏱ TIME ........................................

These eight robots look similar, but they are all in fact different—except for two, which are identical. Can you find the matching pair, then draw a line to join them both?

For each of the three given totals, can you pick one number from each of the rings so that they add up to that total? For example, you could form a total of 14 by picking 2 from the innermost ring, 8 from the middle ring, and 4 from the outermost ring.

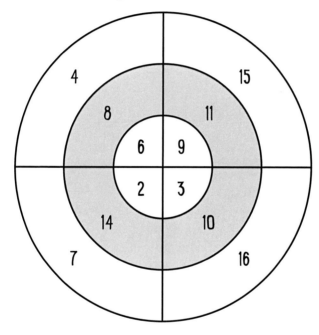

Totals:

19 = _____

25 = _____

34 = _____

Place a number from 1 to 5 into each square so that no number repeats in any row or column. The numbers inside each bold-lined area must add up to the small number printed at the top left of that area.

Take a look at this solved puzzle to see how it works:

| 7+ 3 | 4 | 7+ 2 | 5 | 3+ 1 |
|---|---|---|---|---|
| 6+ 5 | 1 | 14+ 3 | 4 | 2 |
| 7+ 2 | 5 | 4 | 4+ 1 | 3 |
| 5+ 4 | 2 | 1 | 8+ 3 | 5 |
| 1 | 8+ 3 | 5 | 6+ 2 | 4 |

**a)**

**2 3 5**

| 8+ | | 5+ | | 8+ |
|---|---|---|---|---|
| 5+ | | 17+ | 4 | |
| 10+ | | | | |
| | 1 | | 6+ | |
| | 3+ | | 8+ | |

**b)**

**3**
**5**
**1**

| 11+ | 5+ |  | 8+ |  |
|---|---|---|---|---|
|  |  | 6+ |  |  |
| **1** | 9+ |  |  | **5** |
| 9+ |  |  | 10+ |  |
| 7+ |  | 4+ |  |  |

**c)**

**4**
**2**
**3**

| 9+ | 7+ |  | 4+ |  |
|---|---|---|---|---|
|  | 16+ | 4+ |  | 7+ |
| 5+ |  |  |  |  |
|  | 6+ |  |  | 7+ |
| 4+ |  | 6+ |  |  |

Imagine that you cut out and then fold up (bending the paper away from you) the following picture to make a six-sided cube:

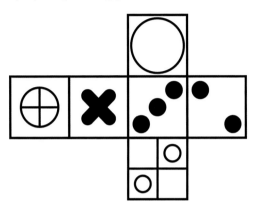

Without actually making the cube, can you say which of the following images would be a possible view of the resulting cube?

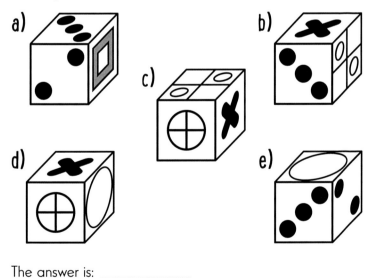

a)

b)

c)

d)

e)

The answer is: ...............................................

How many rectangles, of various sizes, can you count in the following picture? Don't forget the large one all around the outside!

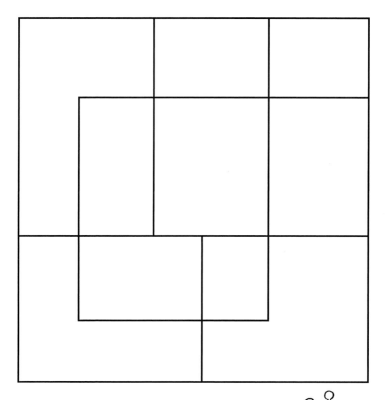

The answer is: ................................

Can you fill in every empty block in each number pyramid so that every square contains a value equal to the sum of the two numbers directly beneath it?

Here's an example to show what a complete pyramid looks like:

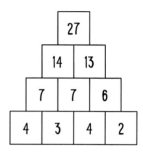

a)

**b)**

| | 63 | 60 | |
| | | 29 |
| 16 | | |
| | | | 7 |

**c)**

| | 45 | 51 | |
| | | 25 |
| 7 | | 10 |
| | | 3 |

Draw along the dashed lines to divide these grids into a complete set of 0 to 6 dominoes so that there is exactly one of each type of domino. Some have already been found, to get you started:

a)

| 0 | 1 | 6 | 0 | 1 | 5 | 3 | 3 |
|---|---|---|---|---|---|---|---|
| 2 | 1 | 4 | 1 | 5 | 5 | 4 | 3 |
| 6 | 6 | 3 | 6 | 2 | 0 | 4 | 6 |
| 0 | 3 | 5 | 1 | 3 | 0 | 0 | 6 |
| 4 | 4 | 6 | 6 | 2 | 4 | 2 | 2 |
| 0 | 2 | 3 | 1 | 4 | 5 | 5 | 1 |
| 0 | 3 | 4 | 5 | 5 | 1 | 2 | 2 |

Use this table to keep track of the dominoes you have already found:

| 0 | 1 | 2 | 3 | 4 | 5 | 6 |   |
|---|---|---|---|---|---|---|---|
|   |   |   |   |   | ✓ |   | 0 |
|   |   |   |   |   |   |   | 1 |
|   |   |   | ✓ |   |   |   | 2 |
|   |   |   |   |   |   |   | 3 |
|   |   |   |   |   |   |   | 4 |
|   |   |   |   |   |   |   | 5 |
|   |   |   |   |   |   |   | 6 |

b)

| 2 | 5 | 1 | 4 | 4 | 4 | 1 | 4 |
|---|---|---|---|---|---|---|---|
| 6 | 0 | 6 | 1 | 1 | 2 | 5 | 6 |
| 1 | 3 | 3 | 1 | 4 | 5 | 2 | 2 |
| 0 | 3 | 5 | 5 | 3 | 0 | 6 | 1 |
| 6 | 1 | 0 | 2 | 3 | 2 | 0 | 0 |
| 6 | 3 | 3 | 4 | 4 | 0 | 5 | 6 |
| 2 | 5 | 2 | 4 | 5 | 3 | 0 | 6 |

Use this table to keep track of the dominoes you have already found:

| | 0 | 1 | 2 | 3 | 4 | 5 | 6 | |
|---|---|---|---|---|---|---|---|---|
| | | | | | | | | 0 |
| | | ✓ | | | | | | 1 |
| | | | | | | | | 2 |
| | | | | | | | | 3 |
| | | | | | | | | 4 |
| | | | | | | | | 5 |
| | | | | | | | | 6 |

Can you find each of these twenty numbers in the grid? They can be written in any direction, including diagonally, and may read forward or backward.

| 148522 | 373540 | 671360 | 928208 |
| 180998 | 4118 | 764287 | 930277 |
| 192465 | 432685 | 806162 | 947414 |
| 233043 | 513766 | 822872 | 951254 |
| 300615 | 530858 | 897601 | 994875 |

| 2 | 5 | 7 | 3 | 3 | 2 | 7 | 9 | 8 | 5 | 7 | 4 | 3 | 6 |
| 3 | 6 | 7 | 7 | 4 | 2 | 7 | 7 | 1 | 9 | 0 | 9 | 4 | 7 |
| 1 | 4 | 0 | 3 | 9 | 8 | 2 | 1 | 2 | 5 | 9 | 1 | 7 | 7 |
| 0 | 2 | 1 | 0 | 2 | 1 | 9 | 9 | 5 | 0 | 1 | 0 | 4 | 7 |
| 6 | 9 | 4 | 4 | 5 | 7 | 8 | 9 | 2 | 8 | 3 | 5 | 8 | 4 |
| 7 | 1 | 6 | 2 | 7 | 1 | 9 | 5 | 7 | 8 | 8 | 9 | 6 | 1 |
| 9 | 7 | 2 | 4 | 2 | 4 | 3 | 7 | 8 | 6 | 2 | 2 | 4 | 9 |
| 8 | 6 | 9 | 0 | 8 | 6 | 9 | 7 | 2 | 0 | 6 | 0 | 5 | 4 |
| 8 | 2 | 1 | 7 | 0 | 2 | 1 | 3 | 6 | 8 | 3 | 0 | 8 | 7 |
| 8 | 3 | 5 | 8 | 7 | 0 | 4 | 6 | 9 | 6 | 2 | 5 | 8 | 8 |
| 1 | 3 | 1 | 4 | 8 | 5 | 2 | 2 | 0 | 4 | 5 | 3 | 7 | 3 |
| 4 | 0 | 8 | 8 | 2 | 2 | 8 | 7 | 2 | 8 | 4 | 6 | 4 | 9 |
| 6 | 4 | 3 | 0 | 0 | 6 | 1 | 5 | 0 | 6 | 3 | 1 | 7 | 6 |
| 7 | 3 | 9 | 4 | 9 | 5 | 1 | 2 | 5 | 4 | 6 | 7 | 9 | 7 |

Take a look at the sequence below, then work out which of the options, *a* to *e*, should replace the empty box to complete the sequence.

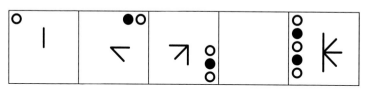

a)

b)

c)

d)

e)

The answer is: ....................................

Draw lines to join each pair of identical shapes, just like in the example solution below. Only one line can enter each square, and lines can't be drawn diagonally.

Here's an example solved puzzle, so you can see how it works:

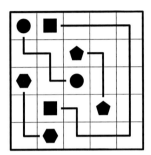

a)

**b)**

**c)**

Each of these two pictures shows the same background image, but in each case different parts of it are covered by white squares. By imagining combining the two pictures, so the empty squares on one are replaced with the corresponding squares from the other picture, can you answer the following questions?

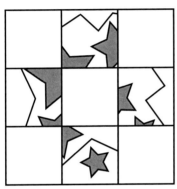

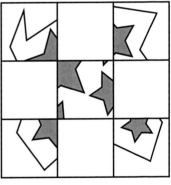

a) How many stars are there in the combined image?

.................................................................................................................................

b) How many sides does the large white polygon have?

.................................................................................................................................

Dan, Emma, Fred and Gia are brothers and sisters. You also know that:

- Dan is two-thirds of Gia's age

- Emma is half of Fred's age

- In eight years' time, Fred will be twice as old as Dan is now

- The youngest of the four is six years old

- None of these brothers and sisters are the same age

Now can you work out how many years old each of the four is? Write your answers in the spaces below:

Dan:
....................................

Emma:
....................................

Fred:
....................................

Gia:
....................................

Write a number from 1 to 4 into each empty square so that no number repeats in any row or column. Numbers must be placed so that whenever there is an inequality arrow between a pair of squares, the arrow always points at the smaller number.

Take a look at this solved example, to see how it works:

| 1 | < | 4 | | 3 | > | 2 |
| 3 | | 2 | | 4 | | 1 |
| 2 | < | 3 | | 1 | | 4 |
| 4 | | 1 | < | 2 | < | 3 |

In the next two puzzles, place a number from 1 to 5 into each empty square:

**c)**

| 4 | | < | | | |
| | 4 | ∨ | | | |
| | | 2 | ^ | < | ∨ |
| ^ | | > | 4 | ∨ | |
| | | < | ^ | 3 | |

**d)**

| | | | | |
| ∨ | 2 | | 4 | < |
| ∨ | | > | | |
| | 1 | | 3 | ^ |
| | | ∨ | | ^ |

Starting on a circle that contains a 1, can you trace a route along the lines to 2, 3, 4 and then 5 in that order, without visiting any number more than once?

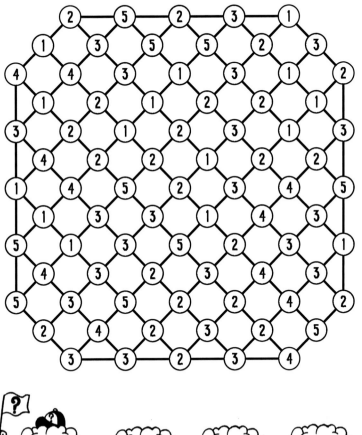

Take a good look at this picture, then when you think you will remember it, turn the page.

Circle the eight changes to the picture. Try to do this without looking back.

If you didn't find them all, look back and try again.

Mike is about to flip a coin. It has "tails" on one side and "heads" on the other.

a) **What is the chance that the coin will show heads on Mike's first coin flip?**

........................................................................................

b) **If Mike flips the coin eight more times, then he might get anywhere from zero to eight tails, but how many is he most likely to get?**

........................................................................................

c) Mike now gets ready to flip the coin two more times. How many—and which—of the following statements is true?

   1) Mike has a 1 in 2 chance of getting first tails and then heads

   2) Mike has a 1 in 4 chance of getting first tails and then heads

   3) Mike has a 1 in 2 chance of getting one tails and one heads in any order

   4) Mike has a 1 in 3 chance of getting the same result both times

........................................................................................

Place either a *0* or a *1* into every empty square, so that every row and column contain equal numbers of each digit. Also, you cannot ever have more than two of the same digit next to each other when reading along a row or column. So *1* and *11* are both okay, but *111* would not be allowed.

Take a look at this example to see how it works. Notice how each row and each column both contain two *1*'s and two *0*'s:

| 0 | 1 | 0 | 1 |
|---|---|---|---|
| 1 | 0 | 0 | 1 |
| 1 | 0 | 1 | 0 |
| 0 | 1 | 1 | 0 |

a)

| 0 |   |   |   |
|---|---|---|---|
| 0 | 0 |   |   |
|   |   | 1 | 0 |
|   |   |   | 0 |

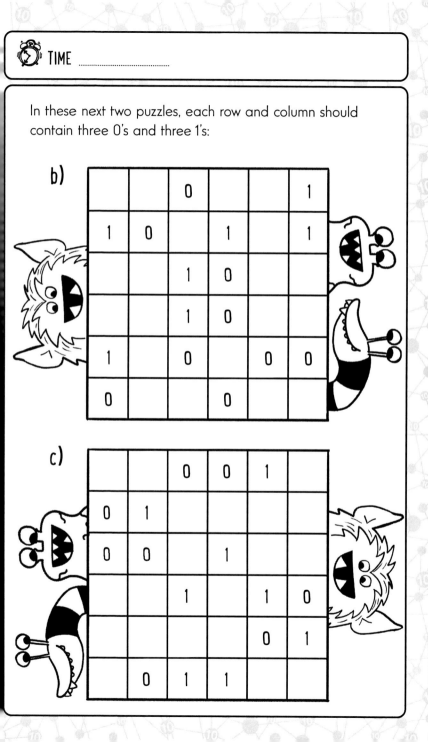

In these next two puzzles, each row and column should contain three 0's and three 1's:

**b)**

| | | 0 | | | 1 |
|---|---|---|---|---|---|
| 1 | 0 | | 1 | | 1 |
| | | 1 | 0 | | |
| | | 1 | 0 | | |
| 1 | | 0 | | 0 | 0 |
| 0 | | | 0 | | |

**c)**

| | | 0 | 0 | 1 | |
|---|---|---|---|---|---|
| 0 | 1 | | | | |
| 0 | 0 | | 1 | | |
| | | 1 | | 1 | 0 |
| | | | | 0 | 1 |
| | 0 | 1 | 1 | | |

Kira, Jade, Iris and Lucy are all knitting new clothes. Each is knitting a different item, and each is using a different shade of wool.

- Kira is knitting a scarf

- The person knitting a hat is using purple wool

- Iris is using green wool

- Jade is not the person knitting socks or a sweater

- The sweater is yellow

- One of the knitters is using blue wool

Can you work out what each person is knitting, and with what wool? Fill out the table below with your deductions:

| Person | Item | Wool Shade |
|---|---|---|
| Kira | | |
| Jade | | |
| Iris | | |
| Lucy | | |

TIME ..........................................

## BRAIN GAME 79

Place all of the given numbers into the grid, crossword-style, so that each number can be read once either across or down. Place one digit per square.

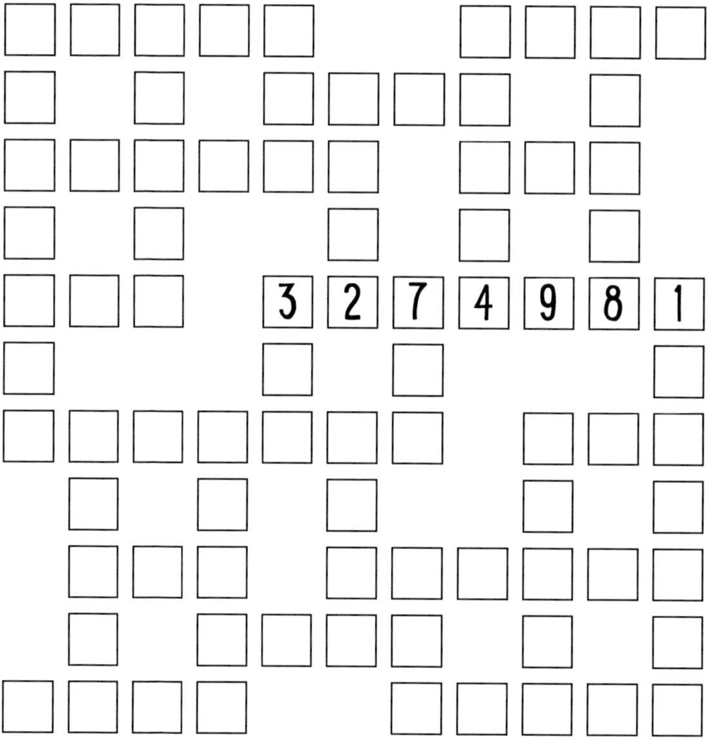


**3 Digits**

171
237
338
367
439
538
757
942

**4 Digits**

1176
1867
3314
3342
3793
7313

**5 Digits**

12922
15945
18948
34989
44997
59213
74464
94618

**6 Digits**

256373
719962

**7 Digits**

1277275
1723549
~~3274981~~
9485817

Write a number into each empty square so that every number from 1 to 16 appears once.

Numbers must be placed so that they form a path from 1 to 16, stepping left/right/up/down from square to square as shown in this example:

| 12 | 13 | 14 | 15 |
|----|----|----|----|
| 11 | 10 | 9  | 16 |
| 6  | 7  | 8  | 1  |
| 5  | 4  | 3  | 2  |

**a)**

| 7  |    | 1  |    |
|----|----|----|----|
|    | 5  |    | 3  |
| 9  |    |    |    |
| 10 |    | 16 |    |

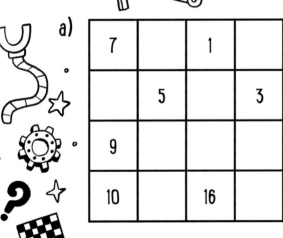

# TIME ........................................

For these next two puzzles, place numbers from 1 to 25:

**b)**

| | 12 | | | |
|---|---|---|---|---|
| 14 | | 22 | 21 | |
| 15 | | 25 | | 7 |
| | 17 | 18 | | 6 |
| | | | 4 | |

**c)**

| 1 | | | 8 | |
|---|---|---|---|---|
| 2 | | | | |
| 3 | | 13 | | 23 |
| | | | | 22 |
| | 18 | | | 21 |

 TIME ........................

Amina is growing a sunflower seed as part of a school project. She plants the seed on the 10th of April, which is a Wednesday. If the seed starts to grow, she should be able to see a green shoot exactly twenty-one days after planting.

a) On what date should Amina see green shoots?

..............................................................................................................................

b) What day of the week will it be?

..............................................................................................................................

c) If the sunflower seed grows well, a flower should first open up eleven weeks after the day on which she planted the seed. If the sunflower opens up exactly on schedule, what will be the date that Amina sees the flower open up?

..............................................................................................................................

..............................................................................................................................

Four views of the same cube are shown here, but one of the faces has been removed on the second cube and replaced with a blank side:

Which of the following five images should replace the blank side to complete the cube correctly?

a)    b)

c)    d)    e)

The answer is: _____

Write a letter from A to H into each empty square so that no letter repeats in any row or column. Also, identical letters cannot be in touching squares—not even diagonally.

Here's an example solved puzzle, to show how it works:

| G | A | E | C | F | H | D | B |
|---|---|---|---|---|---|---|---|
| H | C | D | B | G | E | A | F |
| E | G | F | A | D | C | B | H |
| D | B | C | H | E | A | F | G |
| C | H | A | F | B | G | E | D |
| F | E | B | G | A | D | H | C |
| B | D | H | E | C | F | G | A |
| A | F | G | D | H | B | C | E |

a)

|   | E |   |   |   |   | G |   |
|---|---|---|---|---|---|---|---|
| A |   | G |   |   | B |   | H |
|   | F |   | H | D |   | A |   |
|   |   | C |   |   | E |   |   |
|   |   | F |   |   | H |   |   |
|   | H |   | B | G |   | C |   |
| C |   | A |   |   | F |   | G |
|   | G |   |   |   |   | E |   |

b)

| B |   |   | G | E |   |   | F |
|---|---|---|---|---|---|---|---|
|   |   | B |   |   | C |   |   |
|   | F |   |   |   |   | B |   |
| E |   |   | B | H |   |   | D |
| C |   |   | F | D |   |   | B |
|   | D |   |   |   |   | E |   |
|   |   | F |   |   | H |   |   |
| A |   |   | H | B |   |   | C |

# BRAIN GAME 84 →

Some monsters are hiding in each of these squares. Can you find them all?

- None of the monsters are in the grid squares with numbers.

- There is never more than one monster per grid square.

- Numbers reveal the total number of monsters in all touching squares—including diagonally touching squares.

Look at this solved puzzle
to see how this works:

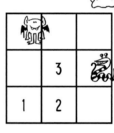

| | | |
|---|---|---|
| | | |
| | 3 | |
| 1 | 2 | |

a)

| 1 | | 2 | |
|---|---|---|---|
| 2 | 3 | | 2 |
| | 2 | | |
| 1 | 1 | 1 | 1 |

b)

| | | | 2 | 2 |
|---|---|---|---|---|
| 2 | | 1 | | |
| | 2 | | 5 | |
| 2 | | | | 4 |
| | 2 | 3 | | |

c)

| 1 | | | 4 | |
|---|---|---|---|---|
| | 3 | | 5 | |
| 1 | | | 4 | |
| 1 | | | 3 | |
| | 1 | 2 | | 2 |

Kat and Liam are both picking flowers from their gardens.

- Kat picks only red flowers, each of which has six petals.

- Liam picks only yellow flowers, each of which has eight petals

Now answer the following questions:

**a)** If Kat picks six red flowers, then how many petals does she have overall in her bunch?

...........................................................................................................................................

**b)** If Liam's bunch of yellow flowers has forty petals in total, then how many flowers has he picked?

...........................................................................................................................................

**c)** If Kat and Liam make a bunch of flowers with exactly the same number of red petals as yellow petals. Which of these options would be one way to make such a bunch?

1. Four red flowers and five yellow flowers

2. Two red flowers and three yellow flowers

3. Four red flowers and three yellow flowers

...........................................................................................................................................

**d)** How many petals would there be, in total, in the bunch chosen in question c3?

...........................................................................................................................................

TIME ..........................................

BRAIN GAME 86

Can you use this decoding table to decipher the strange alien writing below? If you do this correctly you will reveal the names of four well-known singers. Write them in the spaces provided.

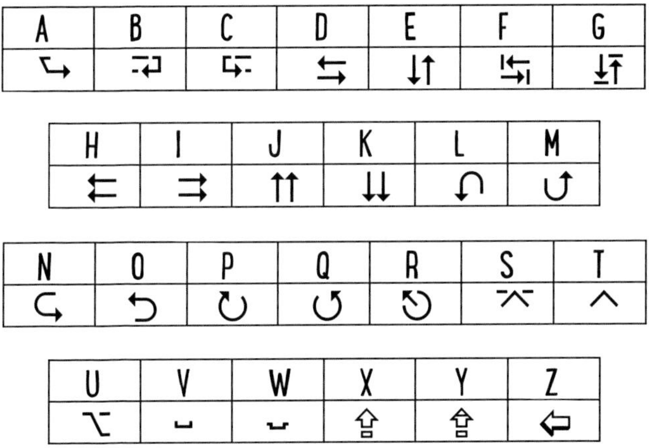

A
B
C
D
E
F
G
H
I
J
K
L
M
N
O
P
Q
R
S
T
U
V
W
X
Y
Z


a) 

..........................................................................................

b) 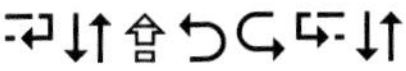

..........................................................................................

c) 

..........................................................................................

d) 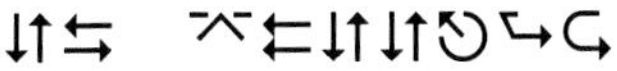

..........................................................................................

Imagine that you have placed
80 bricks to form a 5x4x4 cube,
so they look like this:

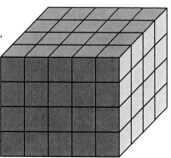

**a)** You then take some bricks away to leave the following
picture. How many bricks remain in this arrangement?
None of them are floating.

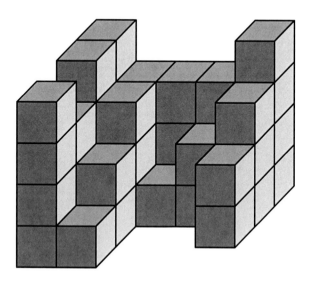

The answer is: ........................................

**b)** You then put all the bricks back so there are 80 of them again. Now you remove some more again to leave the following arrangement. How many bricks are left this time?

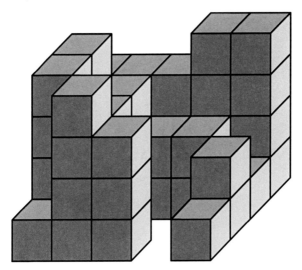

The answer is: ........................................

One of the following images is not like the others. Which one, and why?

**a)**

**b)**

**c)**

**d)**

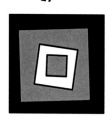

**e)**

**f)**

The answer is: ......................... because ...............................................

.......................................................................................................

The time difference between the cities of Santiago and Auckland is 16 hours. Santiago is behind Auckland's time, so when it's 6 p.m. in Auckland, it's 2 a.m. in Santiago.

a) If it's midday in Santiago on a Wednesday, what time and day is it in Auckland?

..........................................................................................................................................

It takes eleven hours to fly from Auckland to Santiago, or vice-versa.

b) If Sammy leaves Auckland at 6 a.m. local time on a flight to Santiago, what time will it be in Santiago when he arrives?

..........................................................................................................................................

On the return journey, Sammy leaves on a flight from Santiago that departs at 10 a.m. local time, Tuesday.

c) What time and day is it in Auckland when the return flight takes off?

..........................................................................................................................................

d) What time and day is it in Auckland when the return flight lands?

..........................................................................................................................................

..........................................................................................................................................

Write a digit from 1 to 9 into each empty square so that no digit repeats in any row, column or bold-lined 3x3 box.

a)

| | 3 | | 4 | | 2 | | 6 | |
|---|---|---|---|---|---|---|---|---|
| 9 | | | 3 | | 7 | | | 5 |
| | | 8 | | 6 | | 7 | | |
| 3 | 7 | | | | | | 2 | 8 |
| | | 9 | | | | 3 | | |
| 2 | 4 | | | | | | 7 | 6 |
| | | 3 | | 9 | | 6 | | |
| 8 | | | 1 | | 3 | | | 2 |
| | 9 | | 6 | | 4 | | 8 | |

b)

| | | 5 | | 6 | | 9 | | |
|---|---|---|---|---|---|---|---|---|
| | | 9 | 4 | | 2 | 1 | | |
| 1 | 8 | | 3 | | 9 | | 5 | 2 |
| | 1 | 8 | | 3 | | 7 | 4 | |
| 9 | | | 8 | | 7 | | | 3 |
| | 4 | 7 | | 1 | | 5 | 2 | |
| 8 | 7 | | 5 | | 3 | | 6 | 4 |
| | | 3 | 6 | | 4 | 8 | | |
| | | 4 | | 8 | | 3 | | |

Three friends have a bag of treats to share. Inside the bag are four different kinds of treat, which each look different: one type of treat is red, another is orange, a third is yellow, and the fourth type of treat is pink.

Can you use the following clues to work out how many of each type of treat there are in the bag?

- There are enough orange treats for each friend to have exactly three orange treats

- The number of yellow treats is two-thirds of the number of orange treats

- There are twice as many red treats as yellow treats

- If you add together the number of red treats and orange treats, the number is one more than the total of all the pink treats

Write your answers in the spaces below:

Red treats: ............................................

Orange treats: ............................................

Yellow treats: ............................................

Pink treats: ............................................

Total number of treats: ............................

Imagine that you cut out and then fold up each of these images to make four six-sided cubes:

a)

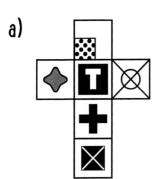

b)

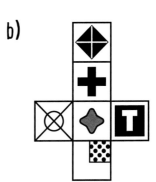

c)

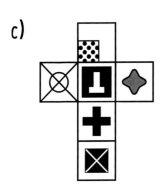

d)

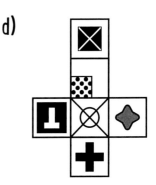

Which one of the options, a to d, would match this completed cube:

The answer is: _____

Write in numbers so that every square contains exactly one number, and each number from 1 to 25 appears once. Every square containing an arrow must point in the direction of the next square in numerical order—although that square might not be a touching square.

Take a look at this example solution to see how it works:

| 1 ↓ | 15 ↓ | 9 ↓ | 20 ↓ | 14 ← |
|---|---|---|---|---|
| 3 ↓ | 22 → | 23 → | 21 ← | 24 ↓ |
| 2 ↑ | 11 → | 10 ← | 19 ↑ | 12 ↓ |
| 4 → | 6 → | 7 ↓ | 5 ← | 13 ↑ |
| 17 → | 16 ← | 8 ↑ | 18 ↑ | 25 |

a)

| 1 → | 3 ↓ | 7 ↓ | 6 ← | ← |
|---|---|---|---|---|
| 23 → | → | ← | ← | 24 ↓ |
| ↓ | ↑ | 10 ← | → | ← |
| 13 → | 15 → | 8 ↓ | ↑ | ← |
| 12 ↑ | → | ↑ | ↑ | 25 |

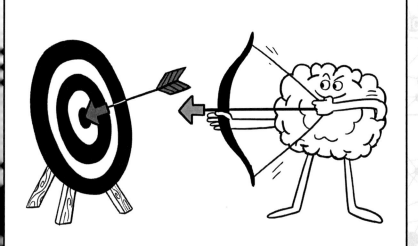

b)

| 1 → | → | ↓ | ↓ | ↓ |
|---|---|---|---|---|
| ↓ | ← | 14 ↓ | ↓ | 3 ↓ |
| 6 → | ↓ | ↑ | 22 ↓ | ← |
| 12 → | 8 ↑ | 13 ↑ | 23 ↓ | ↑ |
| 11 ↑ | ↑ | ← | → | 25 |

Can you draw along some of the dashed lines to divide this shape up into four identical pieces, with no unused parts left over?

Each of the four pieces must be identical, although they can be rotated relative to one another.

Take a look at the solved example, to see how it works.

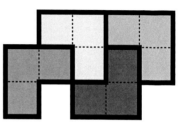

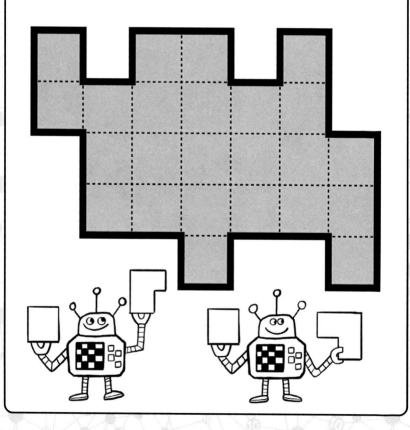

Add a number to each of the following lines so that each line contains a mathematical sequence. The first one is done for you as an example. With the 9 added where shown, the sequence becomes "add 3 at each step."

3    6  *9*  12    15    18    21

a)  87    76    65    43    32    21

b)  10    20    31    56    70    85

c)   2     6    12    20    30    56

d)  901   703   604   505   406   307

Complete each of these jigdoku puzzles by placing a letter from A to G into each empty square. Place letters so that:

- No letter repeats in any row or column

- No letter repeats within any bold-lined shape

This completed puzzle helps show how it works:

| A | G | D | E | B | C | F |
|---|---|---|---|---|---|---|
| E | C | F | D | G | B | A |
| B | D | A | G | F | E | C |
| F | B | G | C | A | D | E |
| G | F | C | B | E | A | D |
| D | E | B | A | C | F | G |
| C | A | E | F | D | G | B |

a)

| E |   | G |   | C |   | D |
|---|---|---|---|---|---|---|
| F |   |   | D |   |   |   |
|   |   | D |   |   | G |   |
| D | F | C |   | E | A | G |
|   | D |   |   | A |   |   |
|   |   | B |   |   |   | C |
| B |   | F |   | G |   | A |

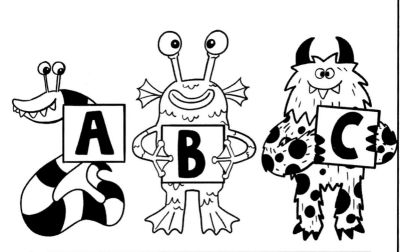

**b)**

| F |   |   |   |   |   | D | A |
|---|---|---|---|---|---|---|---|
|   | F |   |   |   |   |   | B |
|   |   | B | G | C |   |   |   |
|   | A |   | F |   | E |   |   |
|   |   | F | D | A |   |   |   |
| G |   |   |   |   | B |   |   |
| C | D |   |   |   |   |   | E |

Can you fill in every empty block in each number pyramid so that every square contains a value equal to the sum of the two numbers directly beneath it?

Here's an example to show what a complete pyramid looks like:

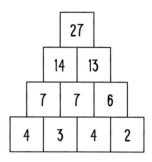

| | 27 | | |
|---|---|---|---|
| | 14 | 13 | |
| | 7 | 7 | 6 |
| 4 | 3 | 4 | 2 |

a)

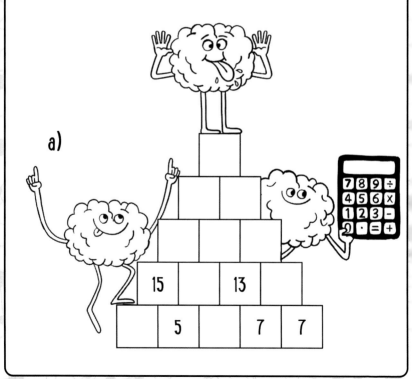

| | 15 | | 13 | |
|---|---|---|---|---|
| | 5 | | 7 | 7 |

b)

| 206 |
| 100 | |
| | | |
| | 27 | |
| 13 | | |
| | | | 7 | 7 |

c)

| | | |
| 65 | | 67 |
| | | 34 |
| | | 17 |
| 9 | 8 | |
| | 5 | |

Place a number from 1 to 5 into each square so that no number repeats in any row or column. The numbers inside each bold-lined area must multiply together to make the small number printed at the top left of that area.

Take a look at this solved puzzle to see how it works:

| 8× 1 | 4 | 30× 2 | 3 | 40× 5 |
|---|---|---|---|---|
| 2 | 3× 1 | 60× 3 | 5 | 4 |
| 60× 5 | 3 | 4 | 4× 1 | 2 |
| 3 | 10× 2 | 5 | 4 | 6× 1 |
| 4 | 5 | 1 | 2 | 3 |

a)

| 5× | | 6× | 8× | |
|---|---|---|---|---|
| 12× | | | 24× | 10× |
| 15× | 1 | 4 | 3 | |
| | | 5× | 4× | |
| 8× | | | 15× | |

**b)**

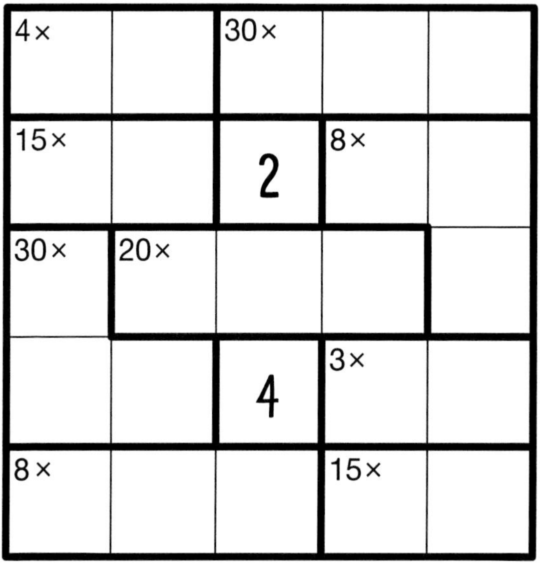

| 4× | | 30× | | |
|---|---|---|---|---|
| 15× | | **2** | 8× | |
| 30× | 20× | | | |
| | | **4** | 3× | |
| 8× | | | 15× | |

**c)**

| 40× | 6× | | 15× | | |
|---|---|---|---|---|---|
| | | 60× | 16× | | |
| | 15× | | | 10× | |
| | | | 12× | | |
| 4× | | | | | |

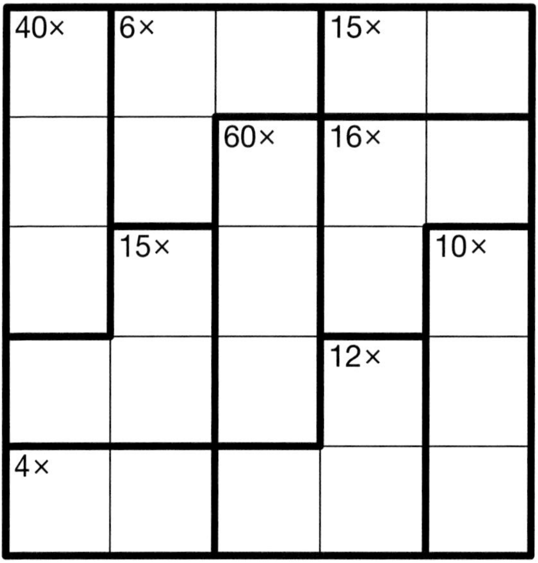

Can you find each of these twenty numbers in the grid? They can be written in any direction, including diagonally, and may read forward or backward.

| | | | |
|---|---|---|---|
| 107882 | 367488 | 630256 | 851502 |
| 165535 | 483037 | 645819 | 922794 |
| 320090 | 548954 | 71192 | 940402 |
| 35110 | 549741 | 717951 | 941709 |
| 364158 | 586729 | 766914 | 963685 |

| 8 | 1 | 6 | 0 | 4 | 1 | 4 | 2 | 0 | 9 | 9 | 6 | 7 | 5 |
|---|---|---|---|---|---|---|---|---|---|---|---|---|---|
| 5 | 5 | 1 | 5 | 8 | 1 | 5 | 9 | 2 | 4 | 4 | 0 | 9 | 0 |
| 1 | 3 | 5 | 7 | 9 | 5 | 0 | 1 | 1 | 8 | 8 | 9 | 9 | 1 |
| 5 | 5 | 5 | 6 | 1 | 0 | 9 | 7 | 7 | 0 | 3 | 9 | 1 | 9 |
| 0 | 7 | 6 | 1 | 2 | 7 | 0 | 1 | 6 | 9 | 0 | 4 | 1 | 1 |
| 2 | 7 | 4 | 3 | 1 | 9 | 9 | 6 | 0 | 6 | 3 | 9 | 7 | 4 |
| 3 | 7 | 9 | 0 | 4 | 0 | 6 | 5 | 3 | 7 | 7 | 5 | 7 | 5 |
| 3 | 6 | 7 | 4 | 8 | 8 | 9 | 0 | 1 | 9 | 8 | 6 | 8 | 9 |
| 5 | 2 | 2 | 8 | 9 | 2 | 7 | 6 | 8 | 5 | 4 | 8 | 3 | 8 |
| 4 | 4 | 2 | 9 | 5 | 0 | 0 | 1 | 3 | 5 | 5 | 0 | 2 | 4 |
| 3 | 6 | 9 | 7 | 9 | 6 | 3 | 6 | 8 | 5 | 3 | 8 | 4 | 5 |
| 5 | 3 | 6 | 4 | 1 | 5 | 8 | 1 | 2 | 0 | 4 | 0 | 4 | 9 |
| 1 | 2 | 9 | 1 | 1 | 7 | 9 | 6 | 3 | 0 | 2 | 5 | 6 | 3 |
| 1 | 6 | 5 | 5 | 3 | 5 | 8 | 1 | 4 | 7 | 9 | 4 | 5 | 8 |

For each of the three given totals, can you pick one number from each of the rings so that they add up to that total? For example, you could form a total of 23 by picking 7 from the innermost ring, 4 from the middle ring, and 12 from the outermost ring.

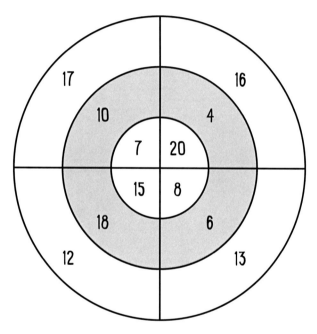

Totals:

32 = ........................................

40 = ........................................

47 = ........................................

You're planning a route across the galaxy, so you can visit all of the amazing planets in the area. Spend a few minutes studying this list of fictional planets in outer space. Once you think you'll remember them all, turn the page and follow the instructions there.

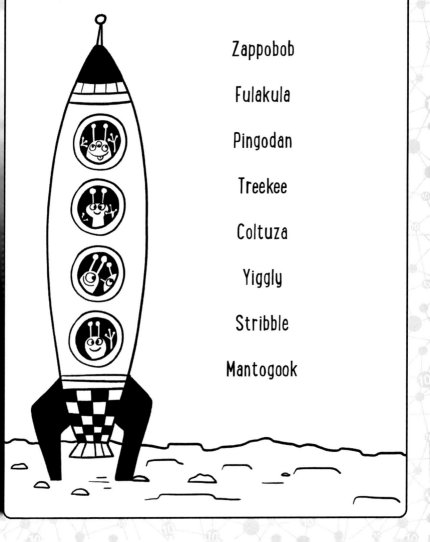

Zappobob

Fulakula

Pingodan

Treekee

Coltuza

Yiggly

Stribble

Mantogook

See if you can rewrite the list of planets below. The first letters are given in the same order, to help you.

Z ........................................

F ........................................

P ........................................

T ........................................

C ........................................

Y ........................................

S ........................................

M ........................................

If you can't remember all the names, repeat the brain game until you have written them all in.

All
of the
ANSWERS

## BRAIN GAME 1

The athletes are:

a) MICHAEL PHELPS
b) USAIN BOLT
c) SIMONE BILES
d) NAOMI OSAKA

---

## BRAIN GAME 2

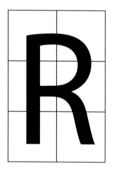

---

## BRAIN GAME 3

a)

b)

| 0 | 3 | 2 | 0 | 4 | 2 |
|---|---|---|---|---|---|
| 0 | 2 | 2 | 4 | 3 | 2 |
| 3 | 4 | 1 | 1 | 1 | 4 |
| 0 | 3 | 1 | 3 | 3 | 4 |
| 0 | 0 | 1 | 2 | 1 | 4 |

# ANSWERS

## BRAIN GAME 4

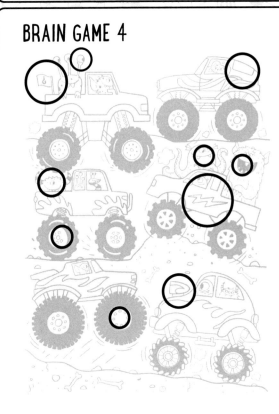

## BRAIN GAME 5

d)

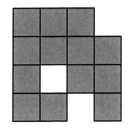

## BRAIN GAME 6

a) 3 coins. You could use two 12k coins to give you 24k, and then add a 3k coin.

b) 6 coins. You could use four 12k coins to give you 48K, then one 3k coin and one 1k coin.

c) 13 coins. You could use:

   5 × 1k coins
   5 × 3k coins
   2 × 10k coins
   1 × 12k coin

## BRAIN GAME 7

a)
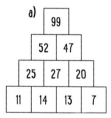

b)
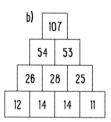

c)
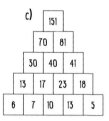

## BRAIN GAME 8

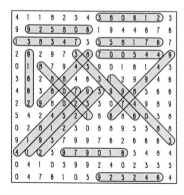

# BRAIN GAME 9

c)—at each step the arrow rotates 90 degrees clockwise while the position of the star moves back and forth between the two bottom corners.

# BRAIN GAME 10

Delete the 0 from the 206 to give: 8 + 18 = 26
Delete the 5 from the 1275 to give: 73 + 54 = 127
Delete either 0 from the 100 to give: 10 × 20 = 200, or delete 0 from 20 to give: 100 x 2 = 200
Delete the 3 from the 1239 to give: 32 + 43 + 54 = 129
Delete the 4 from the 742 to give: 72 ÷ 12 = 6

# BRAIN GAME 11

There are 26 rectangles.

# BRAIN GAME 12

a)

b)

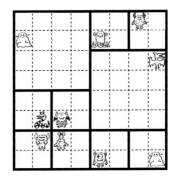

## BRAIN GAME 13

The total along the shortest route is 55.

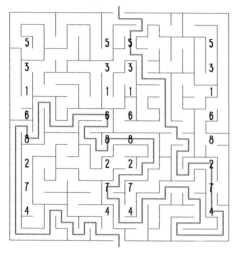

## BRAIN GAME 14

Shape *e* is the odd one out because it is the only image with five circles, whereas all the rest have four circles.

## BRAIN GAME 15

a)

| F | A | D | B | C | E |
|---|---|---|---|---|---|
| B | C | E | A | D | F |
| A | D | F | C | E | B |
| C | E | B | D | F | A |
| D | F | A | E | B | C |
| E | B | C | F | A | D |

b)

| E | F | B | A | C | D |
|---|---|---|---|---|---|
| D | A | C | E | F | B |
| F | E | D | B | A | C |
| C | B | A | F | D | E |
| A | D | E | C | B | F |
| B | C | F | D | E | A |

# BRAIN GAME 16

a) Sunday: Quinn receives the letter on Wednesday, posts one back on Thursday and then Pablo receives it on Sunday.

b) Eleven days: four days for the first letter, the next day to post, then six days to receive one back

c) Friday: eleven days is a week and four days

# BRAIN GAME 17

Arms, Antenna, Laser

# BRAIN GAME 18

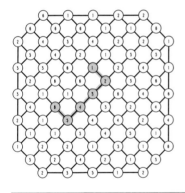

# BRAIN GAME 19

a)
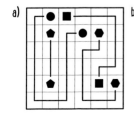

b)
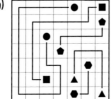

c)
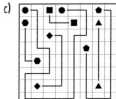

# BRAIN GAME 20

16 = 5 + 9 + 2
26 = 10 + 9 + 7
31 = 13 + 12 + 6

# BRAIN GAME 21

The combined grids look like this:

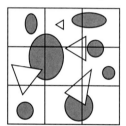

a) 7 ellipses
b) 4 triangles
c) 2 of the triangles overlap ellipses

# BRAIN GAME 22

a)

| 1 | 3 | 2 | 4 | 6 | 5 |
|---|---|---|---|---|---|
| 4 | 6 | 5 | 2 | 3 | 1 |
| 3 | 4 | 1 | 5 | 2 | 6 |
| 5 | 2 | 6 | 1 | 4 | 3 |
| 2 | 5 | 3 | 6 | 1 | 4 |
| 6 | 1 | 4 | 3 | 5 | 2 |

b)

| 1 | 2 | 5 | 4 | 3 | 6 |
|---|---|---|---|---|---|
| 3 | 6 | 4 | 5 | 1 | 2 |
| 2 | 4 | 1 | 3 | 6 | 5 |
| 6 | 5 | 3 | 1 | 2 | 4 |
| 5 | 1 | 6 | 2 | 4 | 3 |
| 4 | 3 | 2 | 6 | 5 | 1 |

c)

| 3 | 1 | 5 | 4 | 2 | 6 |
|---|---|---|---|---|---|
| 2 | 6 | 4 | 5 | 1 | 3 |
| 1 | 5 | 2 | 6 | 3 | 4 |
| 6 | 4 | 3 | 1 | 5 | 2 |
| 5 | 2 | 6 | 3 | 4 | 1 |
| 4 | 3 | 1 | 2 | 6 | 5 |

# BRAIN GAME 23

Cube d is the only possibility. If you position the resulting cube so that the front and top faces match any of a to c then you would have the wrong face on the right-hand side, while cube e has a front face that does not appear on the cube.

# BRAIN GAME 24

Asif is 5, Bobby is 8 and Clara is 4

---

# BRAIN GAME 25

a)

| 1 | 2 | 🐛 | |
| 🐛 | | 4 | 🐛 |
| 2 | 🐛 | 🐛 | 3 |
| | 2 | 3 | 🐛 |

b)

| 1 | 🐛 | 2 | 1 |
| | 3 | 🐛 | 2 |
| 2 | 🐛 | 3 | 🐛 |
| 🐛 | 2 | | 1 |

c)

| 1 | 3 | 🐛 | 4 | 🐛 |
| 🐛 | 🐛 | | 4 | 🐛 |
| 🐛 | | 2 | 4 | 2 |
| 2 | 3 | 🐛 | | 🐛 |
| 🐛 | | 1 | 2 | 1 |

---

# BRAIN GAME 26

Three statements: *b*, *c* and *e*. The other two statements are false.

---

# BRAIN GAME 27

a)

b)

c)

d)

e)

f)

## BRAIN GAME 28

a) 36 bricks: 4 on the top, 7 in the upper middle, 10 in the lower middle, and 15 on the bottom.

b) 27 bricks: 2 on the top, 3 in the upper middle, 8 in the lower middle, and 14 on the bottom.

---

## BRAIN GAME 29

a) Paola is using finger paints
b) Jack is painting a flower
c) Meera is using the acrylic paints

| Person | Picture | Type of Paint |
|--------|---------|---------------|
| Paola | Monster | Finger paints |
| Jack | Flower | Oil |
| Meera | Seashell | Acrylic |

# BRAIN GAME 30

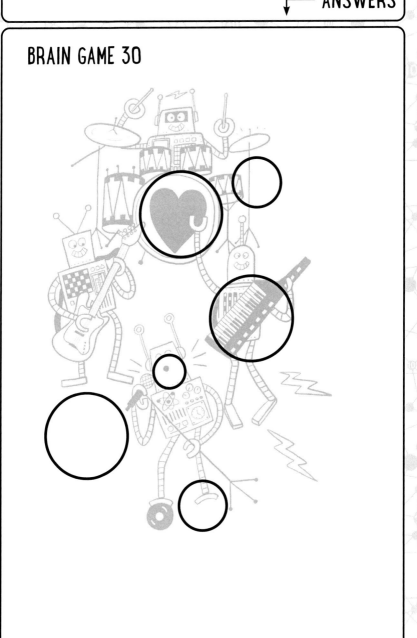

## BRAIN GAME 31

Each letter in the alphabet has been replaced by its numeric position in the alphabet, so A=1, B=2, C=3 and so on. This means that the authors are therefore:

a) ROALD DAHL
b) JUDY BLUME
c) JEFF KINNEY
d) J K ROWLING
e) BEATRIX POTTER

The name BEVERLY CLEARLY should therefore be encoded as 2-5-22-5-18-12-25 3-12-5-1-18-25

---

## BRAIN GAME 32

a)
| 1 ⬇ | 12 ➡ | 4 ⬇ | 13 ⬇ |
| 2 ➡ | 11 ⬆ | 3 ⬆ | 15 ⬇ |
| 8 ⬇ | 7 ⬅ | 6 ⬅ | 14 ⬆ |
| 9 ➡ | 10 ⬆ | 5 ⬆ | 16 |

b)
| 1 ➡ | 10 ⬇ | 2 ⬇ | 15 ⬇ |
| 13 ➡ | 11 ➡ | 12 ⬅ | 14 ⬆ |
| 6 ⬇ | 4 ➡ | 3 ⬅ | 5 ⬅ |
| 7 ➡ | 9 ⬆ | 8 ⬅ | 16 |

## BRAIN GAME 33

a)

| B | G | E | A | C | D | F |
|---|---|---|---|---|---|---|
| E | A | D | F | B | G | C |
| C | F | B | G | A | E | D |
| G | E | C | D | F | B | A |
| F | D | A | B | E | C | G |
| A | B | G | C | D | F | E |
| D | C | F | E | G | A | B |

b)

| A | D | F | B | E | G | C |
|---|---|---|---|---|---|---|
| B | C | E | G | F | D | A |
| F | G | A | D | B | C | E |
| D | E | B | C | A | F | G |
| C | A | D | F | G | E | B |
| G | B | C | E | D | A | F |
| E | F | G | A | C | B | D |

## BRAIN GAME 34

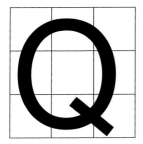

## BRAIN GAME 35

b) The number of swims around the bowl in the opposite direction is a third of the number of clockwise swims

There are 5 half-hour periods in 2.5 hours, so he would make 5x6 = 30 clockwise loops

## BRAIN GAME 36

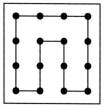

## BRAIN GAME 37

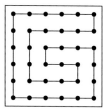

a)

| F | C | D | A | E | B |
|---|---|---|---|---|---|
| B | D | C | F | A | E |
| C | E | A | B | F | D |
| A | F | E | D | B | C |
| D | B | F | E | C | A |
| E | A | B | C | D | F |

b)

| E | A | F | B | D | C |
|---|---|---|---|---|---|
| C | D | A | E | B | F |
| F | C | D | A | E | B |
| B | E | C | F | A | D |
| D | B | E | C | F | A |
| A | F | B | D | C | E |

## BRAIN GAME 38

Option c)

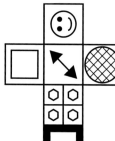

# BRAIN GAME 39

The *?* divides each circled number by 7
The *?* adds 2 and then multiplies by 2 (which is the same as multiplying by 2 and then adding 4)

---

# BRAIN GAME 40

a)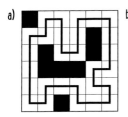

b)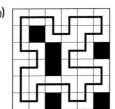

c)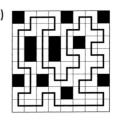

---

# BRAIN GAME 41

a)

| C | D | C | B | A |
|---|---|---|---|---|
| B | D | A | D | C |
| D | A | A | A | B |
| B | C | B | C | D |

b)

| D | C | D | B | C | B | E |
|---|---|---|---|---|---|---|
| E | B | E | E | A | D | C |
| D | B | A | C | E | A | A |
| A | C | A | D | D | B | E |
| B | E | C | C | D | A | B |

c)

| C | A | B | C | A | C | A |
|---|---|---|---|---|---|---|
| D | E | E | D | A | E | B |
| B | D | B | E | C | D | D |
| C | B | E | C | D | E | A |
| D | A | A | B | B | E | C |

## BRAIN GAME 42

a) 4—divide by 4 at each step
b) 131—subtract 19 at each step
c) 1182—add 123 at each step
d) 64—add 9 at each step
e) 720—multiply by 2, then 3, then 4, then 5, then 6
f) 71—prime numbers in descending order

---

## BRAIN GAME 43

*E* is the odd one out because it is the only one where the number of dots does not match the number of sides.

---

## BRAIN GAME 44

a)

| 0 | 0 | 1 | 1 |
|---|---|---|---|
| 0 | 1 | 0 | 1 |
| 1 | 1 | 0 | 0 |
| 1 | 0 | 1 | 0 |

b)

| 0 | 0 | 1 | 0 | 1 | 1 |
|---|---|---|---|---|---|
| 0 | 0 | 1 | 0 | 1 | 1 |
| 1 | 1 | 0 | 1 | 0 | 0 |
| 0 | 1 | 0 | 0 | 1 | 1 |
| 1 | 0 | 1 | 1 | 0 | 0 |
| 1 | 1 | 0 | 1 | 0 | 0 |

c)

| 0 | 0 | 1 | 0 | 1 | 1 |
|---|---|---|---|---|---|
| 0 | 1 | 0 | 1 | 1 | 0 |
| 1 | 0 | 1 | 0 | 0 | 1 |
| 0 | 0 | 1 | 0 | 1 | 1 |
| 1 | 1 | 0 | 1 | 0 | 0 |
| 1 | 1 | 0 | 1 | 0 | 0 |

---

## BRAIN GAME 45

a) 7 a.m.
b) 6 a.m. the next day
c) 15 hours
d) It's 2 p.m. in London and 10 p.m. in Tokyo

## BRAIN GAME 46

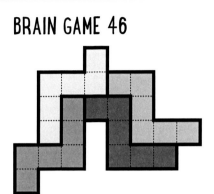

## BRAIN GAME 47

Numbered circles show how many coins you would have left at that stepping stone once you have dropped your coins there

6 coins:

4 coins:

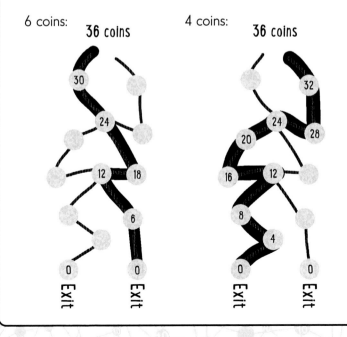

## BRAIN GAME 48

d)

## BRAIN GAME 49

a) December 15th
b) Nine years old
c) Thursday

## BRAIN GAME 50

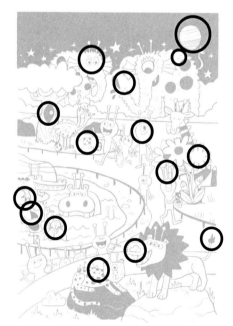

## BRAIN GAME 51

```
 6     9       5 1 9 9 5
9 1 2 3 9 1 8     4     3
   2     1     2 9 2 7 3
4 6 2 2 8     9     4     3
   5     6     5 8 8
9 6 2 4 8     3 1 3 1 7
       4 8 8     3     7
8     8     1     7 9 2 9 7
5 2 4 4 7         6     5
9     5     7 4 2 3 2 8 1
8 5 5 6 1         7     1
```

## BRAIN GAME 52

From top to bottom, the missing entries are as follows:

| | |
|---|---|
| Windows | **6** |
| **Wings** | 5 |
| Satellite launcher | **1** |
| **Airlock doors** | 4 |
| Air tanks | **6** |
| **Alien portals** | 3 |

## BRAIN GAME 53

a) It took Hanna 14 minutes to walk home from school:
- From school to Femi's house took 3 minutes
- From Femi's house to George's house took 6 minutes
- From George's house to Hanna's house took 5 minutes

b) It would take Femi 11 minutes to reach Hanna's house from his house

---

## BRAIN GAME 54

c)

---

## BRAIN GAME 55

a) 203—add 23 at each step
b) 121—divide by 3 at each step
c) 955—subtract 55 at each step
d) 75—the numbers are equal to 100÷1, 100÷2, 100÷3, 100÷4, 100÷5
e) 375—multiply by 5 at each step

## BRAIN GAME 56

a)
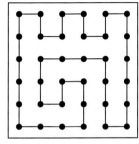

b)
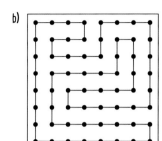

## BRAIN GAME 57

To reveal the name, imagine overlaying the second grid on top of the letter grid so that some of the letters are blocked out. This then reveals the following:

Reading the remaining letters from left to right, top to bottom, the hidden name is therefore ALBERT EINSTEIN, who is probably the most famous scientist of all time.

## BRAIN GAME 58

Bob has three 2b coins, four 5b coins, two 14b coins and a single 20b coin

---

## BRAIN GAME 59

a)

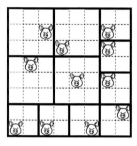

b)

---

## BRAIN GAME 60

a)

| 9 | 7 | 1 | 2 | 8 | 6 | 4 | 3 | 5 |
|---|---|---|---|---|---|---|---|---|
| 3 | 2 | 4 | 7 | 5 | 1 | 8 | 6 | 9 |
| 8 | 6 | 5 | 9 | 4 | 3 | 1 | 7 | 2 |
| 4 | 8 | 7 | 1 | 6 | 5 | 2 | 9 | 3 |
| 6 | 5 | 9 | 3 | 2 | 8 | 7 | 1 | 4 |
| 1 | 3 | 2 | 4 | 7 | 9 | 5 | 8 | 6 |
| 5 | 1 | 8 | 6 | 9 | 2 | 3 | 4 | 7 |
| 2 | 4 | 6 | 8 | 3 | 7 | 9 | 5 | 1 |
| 7 | 9 | 3 | 5 | 1 | 4 | 6 | 2 | 8 |

b)

| 2 | 8 | 9 | 5 | 4 | 6 | 7 | 1 | 3 |
|---|---|---|---|---|---|---|---|---|
| 4 | 6 | 5 | 7 | 1 | 3 | 9 | 2 | 8 |
| 7 | 3 | 1 | 2 | 9 | 8 | 6 | 4 | 5 |
| 3 | 7 | 4 | 9 | 6 | 2 | 5 | 8 | 1 |
| 9 | 5 | 8 | 1 | 7 | 4 | 2 | 3 | 6 |
| 6 | 1 | 2 | 3 | 8 | 5 | 4 | 7 | 9 |
| 1 | 2 | 6 | 8 | 5 | 7 | 3 | 9 | 4 |
| 8 | 4 | 3 | 6 | 2 | 9 | 1 | 5 | 7 |
| 5 | 9 | 7 | 4 | 3 | 1 | 8 | 6 | 2 |

## BRAIN GAME 61

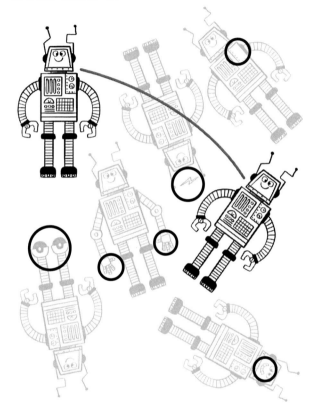

---

## BRAIN GAME 62

19 = 2 + 10 + 7
25 = 2 + 8 + 15
34 = 9 + 10 + 15

# BRAIN GAME 63

**a)**

| | | | | |
|---|---|---|---|---|
| 3 | 5 | 4 | 1 | 2 |
| 2 | 3 | 5 | 4 | 1 |
| 1 | 4 | 2 | 3 | 5 |
| 5 | 1 | 3 | 2 | 4 |
| 4 | 2 | 1 | 5 | 3 |

**b)**

| | | | | |
|---|---|---|---|---|
| 2 | 4 | 1 | 5 | 3 |
| 4 | 5 | 2 | 3 | 1 |
| 1 | 3 | 4 | 2 | 5 |
| 3 | 1 | 5 | 4 | 2 |
| 5 | 2 | 3 | 1 | 4 |

**c)**

| | | | | |
|---|---|---|---|---|
| 4 | 5 | 2 | 3 | 1 |
| 5 | 2 | 3 | 1 | 4 |
| 2 | 4 | 1 | 5 | 3 |
| 3 | 1 | 5 | 4 | 2 |
| 1 | 3 | 4 | 2 | 5 |

# BRAIN GAME 64

Cube *e* is the only possibility. If you position the resulting cube so that the front and top faces match any of *a* to *d*, then you would have the wrong face on the right-hand side.

# BRAIN GAME 65

There are 23 rectangles

# BRAIN GAME 66

**a)**
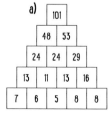

**b)**

**c)**
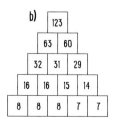

# BRAIN GAME 67

a)

| 0 | 1 | 6 | 0 | 1 | 5 | 3 | 3 |
|---|---|---|---|---|---|---|---|
| 2 | 1 | 4 | 1 | 5 | 5 | 4 | 3 |
| 6 | 6 | 3 | 6 | 2 | 0 | 4 | 6 |
| 0 | 3 | 5 | 1 | 3 | 0 | 0 | 6 |
| 4 | 4 | 6 | 6 | 2 | 4 | 2 | 2 |
| 0 | 2 | 3 | 1 | 4 | 5 | 5 | 1 |
| 0 | 3 | 4 | 5 | 5 | 1 | 2 | 2 |

b)

| 2 | 5 | 1 | 4 | 4 | 4 | 1 | 4 |
|---|---|---|---|---|---|---|---|
| 6 | 0 | 6 | 1 | 1 | 2 | 5 | 6 |
| 1 | 3 | 3 | 1 | 4 | 5 | 2 | 2 |
| 0 | 3 | 5 | 5 | 3 | 0 | 6 | 1 |
| 6 | 1 | 0 | 2 | 3 | 2 | 0 | 0 |
| 6 | 3 | 3 | 4 | 4 | 0 | 5 | 6 |
| 2 | 5 | 2 | 4 | 5 | 3 | 0 | 6 |

# BRAIN GAME 68

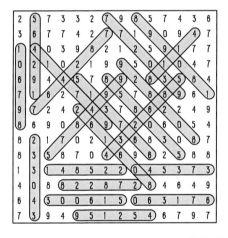

# BRAIN GAME 69

e)—at each step a line is added to the cluster of lines in the middle at 45 degrees clockwise from the most recently added line, and a new circle is added to the line of circles and shaded so that the circles alternate between black and white. Finally, the entire contents of the square is rotated 90 degrees clockwise.

## BRAIN GAME 70

a)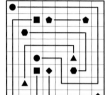
b)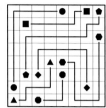
c)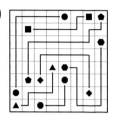

## BRAIN GAME 71

The combined grids look like this:

a) 6 stars
b) 16 sides

## BRAIN GAME 72

Dan is 10, Emma is 6, Fred is 12 and Gia is 15

## BRAIN GAME 73

a)

| 4 > | 3 | 2 > | 1 |
|---|---|---|---|
| 1 < | 2 | 3 (^) | 4 |
| 3 | 4 | 1 | 2 |
| 2 | 1 | 4 > | 3 (^) |

b)

| 3 | 1 | 4 | 2 |
|---|---|---|---|
| 4 (^) | 2 > | 1 | 3 (^) |
| 2 | 4 (^) | 3 | 1 |
| 1 | 3 > | 2 < | 4 |

c)

| 4 | 1 < | 3 | 5 | 2 |
|---|---|---|---|---|
| 3 | 4 | 1 | 2 | 5 |
| 1 | 5 | 2 | 3 (^) < | 4 |
| 2 (^) | 3 | 5 > | 4 | 1 |
| 5 | 2 < | 4 | 1 | 3 (^) |

d)

| 5 | 3 | 2 | 1 | 4 |
|---|---|---|---|---|
| 3 | 2 | 1 | 4 < | 5 |
| 2 | 4 > | 3 | 5 | 1 |
| 4 | 1 | 5 | 3 | 2 (^) |
| 1 | 5 | 4 | 2 | 3 (^) |

## BRAIN GAME 74

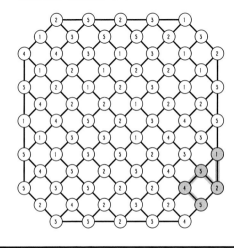

## BRAIN GAME 75

## BRAIN GAME 76

a) 1 in 2, or a half
b) Four
c) Two of the statements are true. There are four possible outcomes: heads-then-tails; heads-then-heads; tails-then-tails; tails-then-heads. Therefore the correct statements are *2* and *3*, and the other two statements are false.

## BRAIN GAME 77

a)

| 0 | 1 | 0 | 1 |
|---|---|---|---|
| 0 | 0 | 1 | 1 |
| 1 | 0 | 1 | 0 |
| 1 | 1 | 0 | 0 |

b)

| 1 | 0 | 0 | 1 | 0 | 1 |
|---|---|---|---|---|---|
| 1 | 0 | 0 | 1 | 0 | 1 |
| 0 | 1 | 1 | 0 | 1 | 0 |
| 0 | 0 | 1 | 0 | 1 | 1 |
| 1 | 1 | 0 | 1 | 0 | 0 |
| 0 | 1 | 1 | 0 | 1 | 0 |

c)

| 1 | 1 | 0 | 0 | 1 | 0 |
|---|---|---|---|---|---|
| 0 | 1 | 0 | 0 | 1 | 1 |
| 0 | 0 | 1 | 1 | 0 | 1 |
| 1 | 0 | 1 | 0 | 1 | 0 |
| 0 | 1 | 0 | 1 | 0 | 1 |
| 1 | 0 | 1 | 1 | 0 | 0 |

## BRAIN GAME 78

| Person | Item | Wool Shade |
|---|---|---|
| Kira | Scarf | Blue |
| Jade | Hat | Purple |
| Iris | Socks | Green |
| Lucy | Sweater | Yellow |

## BRAIN GAME 79

| 1 | 2 | 9 | 2 | 2 |   | 7 | 3 | 1 | 3 |
| 7 |   | 4 |   | 3 | 3 | 1 | 4 |   | 8 |
| 2 | 5 | 6 | 3 | 7 | 3 |   | 4 | 3 | 9 |
| 3 |   | 1 |   |   | 4 |   | 6 |   | 4 |
| 5 | 3 | 8 |   | 3 | 2 | 7 | 4 | 9 | 8 | 1 |
| 4 |   |   |   | 3 |   | 5 |   |   | 2 |
| 9 | 4 | 8 | 5 | 8 | 1 | 7 |   | 3 | 6 | 7 |
|   | 4 |   | 9 |   | 1 |   |   | 4 |   | 7 |
|   | 9 | 4 | 2 |   | 7 | 1 | 9 | 9 | 6 | 2 |
|   | 9 |   | 1 | 8 | 6 | 7 |   | 8 |   | 7 |
| 3 | 7 | 9 | 3 |   |   | 1 | 5 | 9 | 4 | 5 |

## BRAIN GAME 80

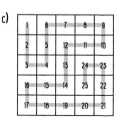

a)

| 7 | 6 | 1 | 2 |
| 8 | 5 | 4 | 3 |
| 9 | 12 | 13 | 14 |
| 10 | 11 | 16 | 15 |

b)

| 13 | 12 | 11 | 10 | 9 |
| 14 | 23 | 22 | 21 | 8 |
| 15 | 24 | 25 | 20 | 7 |
| 16 | 17 | 18 | 19 | 6 |
| 1 | 2 | 3 | 4 | 5 |

c)

| 1 | 6 | 7 | 8 | 9 |
| 2 | 5 | 12 | 11 | 10 |
| 3 | 4 | 13 | 24 | 23 |
| 16 | 15 | 14 | 25 | 22 |
| 17 | 18 | 19 | 20 | 21 |

## BRAIN GAME 81

a) May 1st
b) Wednesday
c) June 26th

# BRAIN GAME 82

a)

---

# BRAIN GAME 83

a)

| B | E | D | C | H | A | G | F |
|---|---|---|---|---|---|---|---|
| A | C | G | E | F | B | D | H |
| E | F | B | H | D | G | A | C |
| H | A | C | G | B | E | F | D |
| G | D | F | A | C | H | B | E |
| F | H | E | B | G | D | C | A |
| C | B | A | D | E | F | H | G |
| D | G | H | F | A | C | E | B |

b)

| B | C | A | G | E | D | H | F |
|---|---|---|---|---|---|---|---|
| H | G | B | D | F | C | A | E |
| D | F | H | C | A | E | B | G |
| E | A | G | B | H | F | C | D |
| C | H | E | F | D | A | G | B |
| F | D | C | A | G | B | E | H |
| G | B | F | E | C | H | D | A |
| A | E | D | H | B | G | F | C |

---

# BRAIN GAME 84

a)

| 1 | 🐙 | 2 | |
|---|---|---|---|
| 2 | 3 | 🐙 | 2 |
| 🐙 | 2 | | 🐙 |
| 1 | 1 | 1 | 1 |

b)

| 🐮 | | | 2 | 2 |
|---|---|---|---|---|
| 2 | | 1 | 🐮 | |
| 🐮 | 2 | | 5 | 🐮 |
| 2 | | 🐮 | 🐮 | 4 |
| 🐮 | 2 | 3 | 🐮 | 🐮 |

c)

| 1 | 👾 | 👾 | 4 | 👾 |
|---|---|---|---|---|
| | 3 | 👾 | 5 | 👾 |
| 1 | | | 4 | |
| 1 | 👾 | | 3 | 👾 |
| | 1 | 2 | 👾 | 2 |

---

# BRAIN GAME 85

a) 36 petals
b) 5 flowers
c) 3—four red flowers and three yellow flowers: 4 x 6 petals
   = 24 petals, and 3 x 8 petals = 24 petals
d) There would be 48 petals in total

## BRAIN GAME 86

Use the table to convert each symbol into the corresponding letter, to reveal the six singers:

HARRY STYLES
BEYONCE
TAYLOR SWIFT
ED SHEERAN

---

## BRAIN GAME 87

a) 42 bricks: 4 on the top, 10 in the upper middle, 13 in the lower middle, and 15 on the bottom
b) 47 bricks: 5 on the top, 11 in the upper middle, 14 in the lower middle, and 17 on the bottom

---

## BRAIN GAME 88

Shape *f* is the odd one out because all the others have exactly one white shape, one black shape and two grey shapes.

# BRAIN GAME 89

a) 4 a.m. on Thursday—the next day.

b) 1 a.m. The flight takes eleven hours, so the time is 5 p.m. in Auckland when the plane lands—but Santiago is sixteen hours behind this time, making it 1 a.m. in Santiago. As far as the calendar is concerned, Sammy will have gone back in time, since he left Auckland at 6 a.m. and arrived at 1 a.m. on the same day!

c) 2 a.m. on Wednesday

d) 1 p.m. on Wednesday

# BRAIN GAME 90

a)

| 5 | 3 | 7 | 4 | 1 | 2 | 8 | 6 | 9 |
|---|---|---|---|---|---|---|---|---|
| 9 | 6 | 4 | 3 | 8 | 7 | 2 | 1 | 5 |
| 1 | 2 | 8 | 5 | 6 | 9 | 7 | 3 | 4 |
| 3 | 7 | 1 | 9 | 4 | 6 | 5 | 2 | 8 |
| 6 | 8 | 9 | 7 | 2 | 5 | 3 | 4 | 1 |
| 2 | 4 | 5 | 8 | 3 | 1 | 9 | 7 | 6 |
| 4 | 1 | 3 | 2 | 9 | 8 | 6 | 5 | 7 |
| 8 | 5 | 6 | 1 | 7 | 3 | 4 | 9 | 2 |
| 7 | 9 | 2 | 6 | 5 | 4 | 1 | 8 | 3 |

b)

| 4 | 2 | 5 | 1 | 6 | 8 | 9 | 3 | 7 |
|---|---|---|---|---|---|---|---|---|
| 7 | 3 | 9 | 4 | 5 | 2 | 1 | 8 | 6 |
| 1 | 8 | 6 | 3 | 7 | 9 | 4 | 5 | 2 |
| 6 | 1 | 8 | 2 | 3 | 5 | 7 | 4 | 9 |
| 9 | 5 | 2 | 8 | 4 | 7 | 6 | 1 | 3 |
| 3 | 4 | 7 | 9 | 1 | 6 | 5 | 2 | 8 |
| 8 | 7 | 1 | 5 | 9 | 3 | 2 | 6 | 4 |
| 5 | 9 | 3 | 6 | 2 | 4 | 8 | 7 | 1 |
| 2 | 6 | 4 | 7 | 8 | 1 | 3 | 9 | 5 |

# BRAIN GAME 91

Red = 12 treats

Orange = 9 treats

Yellow = 6 treats

Pink = 20 treats

Total = 47 treats

## BRAIN GAME 92

a)

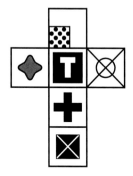

---

## BRAIN GAME 93

a)

| 1 → | 3 ↓ | 7 ↓ | 6 ← | 2 ← |
|---|---|---|---|---|
| 23 → | 20 → | 22 ← | 21 ← | 24 ↓ |
| 11 ↓ | 19 ↑ | 10 ← | 17 → | 18 |
| 13 → | 15 → | 8 ↓ | 16 ↑ | 14 ← |
| 12 ↑ | 4 → | 9 ↑ | 5 ↑ | 25 |

b)

| 1 → | 19 → | 16 ↓ | 20 ↓ | 2 ↓ |
|---|---|---|---|---|
| 10 ↓ | 9 ← | 14 ↓ | 21 ↓ | 3 ↓ |
| 6 → | 7 ↓ | 15 ↑ | 22 ↓ | 5 ← |
| 12 → | 8 ↑ | 13 ↑ | 23 ↓ | 4 ↑ |
| 11 ↑ | 18 ↑ | 17 ← | 24 → | 25 |

## BRAIN GAME 94

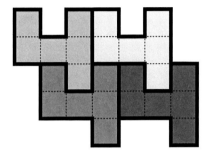

## BRAIN GAME 95

a) Insert *54* after the third number to form the sequence
   "subtract 11 at each step":
   - 87, 76, 65, **54**, 43, 32, 21

b) Insert *43* after the third number to form the sequence
   "add 10, then 11, then 12, then 13, then 14, then 15":
   - 10, 20, 31, **43**, 56, 70, 85

c) Insert *42* after the fifth number to form the sequence
   "1×2, 2×3, 3×4, 4×5, 5×6, 6×7, 7×8" (which is the same as
   "add 4, then 6, then 8, then 10, then 12, then 14"):
   - 2, 6, 12, 20, 30, **42**, 56

d) Insert *802* after the first number to form the sequence
   "subtract 99 at each step":
   - 901, **802**, 703, 604, 505, 406, 307

## BRAIN GAME 96

a)

| E | B | G | A | C | F | D |
|---|---|---|---|---|---|---|
| F | G | A | C | D | B | E |
| C | A | D | E | B | G | F |
| D | F | C | B | E | A | G |
| G | D | E | F | A | C | B |
| A | E | B | G | F | D | C |
| B | C | F | D | G | E | A |

b)

| F | G | C | E | B | D | A |
|---|---|---|---|---|---|---|
| D | F | G | C | E | A | B |
| A | E | B | G | C | F | D |
| B | A | D | F | G | E | C |
| E | B | F | D | A | C | G |
| G | C | E | A | D | B | F |
| C | D | A | B | F | G | E |

## BRAIN GAME 97

a)
```
      101
    50   51
  26   24   27
 15  11  13  14
10  5   6   7   7
```

b)
```
       206
     100  106
   49   51   55
  25  24  27  28
 14  11  13  14  14
9   5   6   7   7   7
```

c)
```
        264
      131  133
    65   66   67
   32  33  33  34
  15  17  16  17  17
 6  9  8  8  9  8
2  4  5  3  5  4  4
```

## BRAIN GAME 98

a)
| 3+ 1 | 5 | 6+ 3 | 8+ 2 | 4 |
|---|---|---|---|---|
| 12+ 4 | 3 | 2 | 24+ 1 | 10+ 5 |
| 15+ 5 | 1 | 4 | 3 | 2 |
| 3 | 2 | 3+ 5 | 4+ 4 | 1 |
| 8+ 2 | 4 | 1 | 15+ 5 | 3 |

b)
| 4+ 1 | 4 | 50+ 3 | 2 | 5 |
|---|---|---|---|---|
| 15+ 5 | 3 | 2 | 8+ 1 | 4 |
| 30+ 3 | 1 | 20+ 5 | 4 | 2 |
| 2 | 5 | 4 | 3+ 3 | 1 |
| 8+ 4 | 2 | 1 | 15+ 5 | 3 |

c)
| 40+ 4 | 6+ 2 | 1 | 15+ 5 | 3 |
|---|---|---|---|---|
| 2 | 3 | 40+ 5 | 18+ 1 | 4 |
| 5 | 15+ 1 | 3 | 4 | 10+ 2 |
| 3 | 5 | 4 | 12+ 2 | 1 |
| 4+ 1 | 4 | 2 | 3 | 5 |

## BRAIN GAME 99

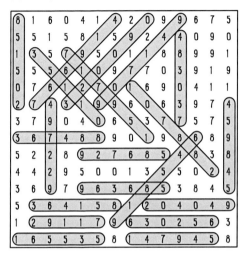

## BRAIN GAME 100

32 = 15 + 4 + 13
40 = 20 + 4 + 16
47 = 20 + 10 + 17

# BRAIN GAME 101

Z appobob

F ulakula

P ingodan

T reekee

C oltuza

Y iggly

S tribble

M antogook

# NOTES AND SCRIBBLES

# Also available from Ulysses Press: